CAPSTONE

SUCCEEDING BEYOND COLLEGE

Robert M. Sherfield
THE COMMUNITY COLLEGE OF SOUTHERN NEVADA

Rhonda J. Montgomery
THE UNIVERSITY OF NEVADA, LAS VEGAS

Patricia G. Moody
THE UNIVERSITY OF SOUTH CAROLINA

Prentice
Hall

Upper Saddle River, New Jersey 07458

Library of Congress Cataloging-in-Publication Data

Sherfield, Robert M.
    Capstone : succeeding beyond college / Robert M. Sherfield, Rhonda J. Montgomery,
Patricia G. Moody.
       p.   cm.
    Includes bibliographical references and index.
    ISBN 0-13-086613-0
    1. Vocational guidance—United States.   2. Job hunting—United States.   3.
School-to-work transition—United States.   4. College graduates—Employment—United
States.   5. College graduates—United States—Interviews.   I. Montgomery, Rhonda J.   II.
Moody, Patricia G.   III. Title.

HF5382.5.U5 S468 2001
650.14—dc21

                                        00-058884

Acquisitions Editor: Sande Johnson
Assistant Editor: Michelle Williams
Production Editor: Holcomb Hathaway
Director of Manufacturing and Production: Bruce Johnson
Managing Editor: Mary Carnis
Manufacturing Manager: Ed O'Dougherty
Art Director: Marianne Frasco
Marketing Manager: Jeff McIlroy
Marketing Assistant: Barbara Rosenberg
Cover Design: Lorraine Castellano
Cover Art: Shakirov, SIS/Images.com
Composition: Aerocraft Charter Art Service
Printing and Binding: R. R. Donnelly

Prentice-Hall International (UK) Limited, *London*
Prentice-Hall of Australia Pty. Limited, *Sydney*
Prentice-Hall Canada Inc., *Toronto*
Prentice-Hall Hispanoamericana, S.A., *Mexico*
Prentice-Hall of India Private Limited, *New Delhi*
Prentice-Hall of Japan, Inc., *Tokyo*
Pearson Education Singapore Pte. Ltd.
Editora Prentice-Hall do Brasil, Ltda., *Rio de Janeiro*

10 9 8 7 6 5 4 3 2 1

ISBN 0-13-086613-0

Brief Contents

UNIT THREE

Life and Personal Enrichment   155

Contents

CHAPTER 3   The Resume and Career Portfolio   25

CHAPTER 4   Professional Presence   37

CHAPTER 5   Professional Communication   51

UNIT TWO

Professional Development   81

CHAPTER 7   Diversity in the Workplace   83

CHAPTER 8   Workplace Politics and Civility   91

UNIT THREE

Life and Personal Enrichment **155**

About the Authors

Robert Sherfield is Co-Director of the Faculty Center for Learning and Teaching and a Professor in the Department of English at the Community College of Southern Nevada in Las Vegas. For more than 15 years, he has been a nationally recognized speaker, trainer, and consultant.

An award-winning educator, Robb was recently named Outstanding Faculty of the Year at CCSN. He twice received the Distinguished Teacher of the Year Award from the University of South Carolina and has received numerous other awards and nominations for outstanding classroom instruction and advisement. In 1998, 1999, and 2000 he was nominated for and named in *Who's Who Among American Educators*. He has co-authored textbooks and trade books including *Cornerstone: Building on Your Best (First, Second, and Concise Editions), Roadways to Success,* and *365 Things I Learned in College.*

Robert also has conducted workshops and keynote addresses for more than 100 institutions of higher education and education associations across the United States including the National Association of Developmental Education, the College Reading and Learning Association, and the South Carolina Technical Education Association.

Rhonda Montgomery is an Associate Professor in the William F. Harrah College of Hotel Administration, University of Nevada, Las Vegas. Her research and teaching

interests include private-club management, meetings, conventions, and exposition management, and college success strategies.

Rhonda received the Distinguished Teacher of the Year Award, the highest honor from her students and colleagues at the University of South Carolina. Rhonda also has received the Faculty of the Month Award from the University of Nevada, Las Vegas and numerous awards for her work with advising and mentoring students.

Rhonda has authored and co-authored numerous textbooks including *Cornerstone: Building on Your Best (First, Second, and Concise Editions)*, *A Club Manager's Guide to Private Parties and Club Functions*, and *Meetings, Conventions and Expositions: An Introduction to the Industry*. She is a contributing author to the club management textbook *Contemporary Club Management*.

Pat Moody is Dean of the College of Hospitality, Retail and Sport Administration at the University of South Carolina, where she has been on the faculty for nearly 25 years. Pat has been honored as Distinguished Educator  of the Year at her college, Collegiate Teacher of the Year by the National Business Education Association, and a top-five finalist for the Amoco Teaching Award at the University of South Carolina. In 1994, she was awarded the prestigious John Robert Gregg Award, the highest honor in her field of more than 100,000 educators.

A nationally known motivational speaker, Pat has spoken in 42 states and several foreign countries. Frequently she keynotes national and regional conferences and has given her signature presentation, *Fly Like An Eagle,* to thousands of people including the 1984 Olympic Athletes.

Pat is an avid sports fan. She enjoys spending time at the beach and with her two grandchildren, Jackson and Lauren.

A Message to Our Students

ollectively, we bring to this project almost 50 years of experience in teaching, advising, coaching, tutoring, and administration. Over the years, we have found joy and comfort in helping our students select and pursue careers in the fields of their dreams.

On many occasions, however, we have watched talented, gifted students turned away from prestigious jobs, companies, and institutions because of their careless, and sometimes unknown, errors in writing, interviewing, and social graces. This is the reason for our interest in and passion for the *Capstone* project. We hope that, as you read this book, you will come to understand more about the world of work, writing a resume, networking and making professional contacts, putting your senior-year portfolio to use, interviewing, workplace politics, leadership, post-college finances, and discovering more about what you have to offer the world.

Each unit opens with a personal story from a recent graduate. This feature, *Advice From a Peer,* will help you understand more about the transition from college to the world of work. When interviewing these former students, we asked them to paint a realistic picture and to be honest. We think their advice will greatly assist you.

Another feature of each chapter is *Advice From a Mentor.* We went into the fields of business, education, medicine, law, consulting, hospitality, convention management, marketing, finance, and banking to find professionals who would offer their best advice about success. We hope you find their contributions as interesting, educational, and inspirational as we did.

Whatever your age, your goals, your dreams, or your passion, we hope that our words, advice, and encouragement will strengthen your senior year, your understanding of the world of work, and your commitment to making a valued contribution to humanity.

All the best to you,

Robb, Rhonda, and Pat

Dedication

To Dr. Marilyn C. Kameen

Had it not been for you, our paths never would have crossed.
Thank you for a most wonderful, unexpected gift!

Acknowledgments

Robert Silverman, Interim President, Community College of Southern Nevada; Theo Byrns, Associate Vice President, Community College of Southern Nevada; Don Smith, Dean of Arts and Letters, Community College of Southern Nevada; Charles Mosley, Chair, Department of English, Community College of Southern Nevada; Carol Harter, President, University of Nevada, Las Vegas; Stuart Mann, Dean, College of Hotel Administration, University of Nevada, Las Vegas; Patti Shock, Department Chair, University of Nevada, Las Vegas; John Palms, President, University of South Carolina; Jerome Odom, Provost, University of South Carolina; Joan Dominik, Kennesaw State University; Steve Stricker, University of Mississippi; Eileen McGarry, University of Nevada, Las Vegas; Vincent DiSano, Syracuse University

Our colleagues and friends: Wanda Daniel, Lucinda Moyano, Garcia Tate, Maritza Correa, Steve Brannon, Bryan Delph, James Farmer, Javier Ortiz, Joanna Hibler, Charles Goodwin, Joe Perdue, Curtis Roe, Tim Rice, Martin Schwartz, Steve Spearman

Our students: Kevin Todd Houston, Chris Latusky, Dana Bennett

And a special thanks to: Brian Epps, Mick Montgomery, Jackie Montgomery, Wallace Moody, Wyck Moody and family, and Mike Moody and family.

CAPSTONE

SUCCEEDING BEYOND COLLEGE

UNIT ONE

Preparing for the WWW

(THAT'S THE WONDERFUL WORLD OF WORK)

ADVICE FROM A PEER

Dr. Kevin Todd Houston,

Graduate, Speech and Language Pathology,
The University of South Carolina, Columbia

My career has been a strange one. I began my first year of college with a major in
Photo Journalism. Nothing interested me more than talking to the world through photography. I worked for a local, small, daily newspaper while attending college. After
graduating, I began working at the state's largest newspaper. But something was

wrong. There was a hole in my professional life, and I couldn't imagine why. I had my dream job—or so I thought.

While working for the paper, I met a great friend who happened to have a hearing impairment. I was amazed at how much I enjoyed learning to communicate with him, but I also was afraid. Something was brewing in me. It was a new desire—a desire far from my first love, photography—so far from all of the coursework, exams, and previous studies. This couldn't be happening!

Finally I gave in to my deep-seeded desire to learn more about speech and language pathology, and I began to pursue my master's degree in a totally different area. Before I knew it, I was in love with another profession. I know that this is not common, but it does happen more than you might think.

Am I telling you to change your major, to quit your job, to rethink your life's plan? No. But I am suggesting that if you find yourself working in a field that is not your passion, you should think strongly about the next 40 years of your life. Are you going to spend them doing something that does not bring you joy?

I recently graduated, and today I hold a Ph.D. in Speech and Language Pathology and teach at the University of South Carolina. I found my passion. I found my dream. I found my home! I wish you luck in finding yours.

CHAPTER 1

From Backpacks to Briefcases

Far better is it to dare mighty things, to win glorious triumphs, even though checkered with failure, than to take rank with those poor spirits who neither enjoy much, nor suffer much, because they live in the gray twilight that knows not victory, nor defeat!

F. D. ROOSEVELT

This is it—quite possibly the moment you've waited for all of your life! You are beginning your last semester in college. This is the moment dreams are made of. You may be going on to graduate school, volunteering with the Peace Corps, or entering the wonderful world of work. Regardless, in a few short months your life is going to change drastically. Close friends will scatter across the nation, dorm rooms will become a thing of the past and, believe it or not, you will miss the opportunity to sit and read a play with friends, discuss the thoughts of Nietzsche over pizza, or ponder Galileo's astronomy while walking home from night classes. Don't be sad, though. Your glorious triumphs are at hand.

Capstone: Succeeding Beyond College is intended to be a guide for you. As we begin this journey together, we want you to know that the words, advice, and suggestions offered here come from years of hard work, continuing education, industry and business contacts, and trial and error. We hope that during the journey of *Capstone,* you are able to develop a map to help you navigate through the challenging days and months to come. During this journey we will have the opportunity to share our insights on topics such as building a dynamic resume, communicating professionally, dressing for success, delivering a vibrant interview, celebrating diversity, working with committees, managing meetings, solving conflicts, discovering your leadership talents, maximizing your potential, managing your finances, and creating balance and harmony in your life.

This chapter will deal with suggestions and tips for making the transition from college to career. To give you time to reflect on who you are and what you have to offer, this chapter will discuss the following topics:

▲ A different kind of workforce

▲ Identifying skills to help you succeed in the workplace such as:

writing, speaking, and listening skills	teamwork
loyalty and trustworthiness	a strong work ethic
confidence and decision-making skills	professionalism
priority management skills	computer literacy
the ability to change and grow	critical thinking skills
human relationship skills	multi-tasking

▲ Knowing yourself

The Workforce of the 21st Century

According to Richard Nelson Bolles, author of the multi-million-dollar bestseller, *What Color Is Your Parachute?* (1994), "There's a whole lot of shakin' goin' on." He refers to today's workplace as the "workquake" and suggests that the world's workplace is going through major restructuring. In the 1994 edition of his book, he listed eight characteristics of the workplace:

- Debt everywhere
- Downsizing
- Pessimism
- More hours
- Smaller paychecks
- Lower standard of living
- More part-time work
- Less job security

This is not a very pretty picture, is it? Take heart. These characteristics are not mentioned in the 1999 version of *What Color Is Your Parachute?*. Instead, much discussion is given to finding a job through the Internet. That picture, however, is a shocking one to say the least. Bolles states that one job listing site alone had "85,000 resumes, but only 850 employers even looked at them over a period of three months."

So why are we telling you all of this? Why would we begin a chapter (and a book) with such gloom and doom? The answer is simple. There are ways to combat these characteristics and shocking Internet numbers. There are ways to avert a career-search disaster. By paying close attention to the discussion in the following pages and chapters, you will begin to understand how to get the edge you so desperately need in today's ever-changing marketplace.

Establishing and Refining Yourself in Today's "Workquake"

College graduates are a dime a dozen. This does not mean, however, that *you* are a dime a dozen. Herein lies the challenge. How do you distinguish yourself from the countless job-seekers out there? What are you going to do that sets you apart from your competition? What do you have to offer that no one else can possibly offer to an employer? We will discuss some of the talents and qualities that are becoming increasingly rare, yet constantly sought after, in today's "workquake." By understanding more about these qualities, you will put yourself miles ahead of the competition.

▲ ▲ ▲

WRITING, SPEAKING, AND LISTENING SKILLS

As you read this book, you may think that we are beating a dead horse. Again and again, in almost every chapter, we offer some type of advice, suggestion, or tip for becoming a more effective written, verbal, and nonverbal communicator. We do so because these are constantly listed as top skills needed for success. We do so because so few people actually possess these qualities. If you want to put yourself ahead of the competition, attend every class, every seminar, every meeting, and every function where you can learn more about effective writing, speaking, and listening skills. Chapters 5 and 15 deal specifically with these skills.

ΛDVIƇΣ FRØM Λ MΣNTØR

Wanda Daniel, Ed.D.,

Consultant and Personal Development Trainer, Impression Management International, Atlanta, GA

▲ ▲ ▲

A STRONG WORK ETHIC

I am motivated by new technology. You won't hear many people from my generation say that, but I love the challenge of learning something new. As a trainer and consultant, can you imagine the reaction if I were to approach potential clients and tell them that I want to conduct a training session on WordPerfect 2.0 or DOS applications? I would be laughed out of the office. Keeping current, learning, and growing are essential to my business, and these qualities will be essential to your success in today's workplace.

For more than 30 years, my father worked in the textile industry in South Carolina. During my entire life, I remember him missing only two days of work—when his father died. I watched him work when he was sick, tired, and

Throughout my several different, yet related, careers, I have recharged by studying areas that were new and exciting to me. Going back to school or taking additional courses have been energizers. The courses usually did not even relate to what I was doing professionally at the moment. However, what I was learning eventually allowed me to parlay my skills into several exciting and lucrative positions, including Convention Manager for a national association and an International Consultant and Trainer.

drained. That was the way he was raised: You take a job, you commit to that job, and you report to that job when you are supposed to. Biased though I may be by my father's work ethic, I would wager that not many people maintain his position on work. That may be good.

Most medical and scientific research suggests that working while sick and working under immense stress can be detrimental to overall health. Contrary to popular belief, most employers don't want you to work yourself to death. In today's environment, however, they do want to make sure they get every penny's worth they pay you. Our suggestion is to develop a strong work ethic that is healthy for you and your employer. Working yourself into sickness or even death will not serve anyone in the long run.

▲ ▲ ▲

LOYALTY AND TRUSTWORTHINESS

Today, competition is strong among companies vying for the same customers. In some instances you have to sign a legal document forbidding you from discussing or sharing your work with any-one. Some industries also ask for a non-compete clause. If you leave Company X, this clause prohibits you from working for Company Y, and sometimes within the same industry, for six months to one year, maybe even longer.

In this light, loyalty to your employer is a highly regarded trait. Loyalty, however, cannot be mea-sured by a resume or determined by a simple interview. Proving that you have loyalty and are trustworthy comes over time. It may take years to establish these characteristics with your company and within your industry but, be warned, it takes only seconds to destroy what took years to create.

▲ ▲ ▲

TEAMWORK

Employers are looking for people who not only understand the concept of teamwork but also excel and participate in teamwork. A

ΛDVIϾƐ
CONTINUED.

One of the best pieces of advice ever given to me was this: "Never be satisfied." Now, that can be taken many differ-ent ways, but I took it to mean that I had to keep up with the times or I would be left behind. How true that has been. Take it from someone who grew up without computers—I couldn't survive in today's world if I had been satisfied with knowing only what I learned 20 years ago.

As you enter the workforce, I encourage you to learn all you can, be the best you can be, stretch yourself to the limits, take risks, and learn to predict change. Your career will be all the better because of these activities.

humorous cartoon figure says, "Teamwork is a bunch of people doing what I say!" Unfortunately, many people think this *is* teamwork. A true team has shared responsibilities, shared purposes, shared goals, shared visions, and, most important, shared accountability.

Team players understand that successful and efficient teamwork involves listening to each other, respecting each other, supporting each other, lifting up each other in times of trouble, working together to resolve conflicts quickly, making each other look good, and, ultimately, bringing your personal best to the table each and every time you meet. If you strive to be a team player, you will quickly reap the benefits.

▲ ▲ ▲

PROFESSIONALISM

The term *professionalism* varies from workplace to workplace. What is professional for one office or setting may be totally inappropriate for another. This includes everything from language use to clothing to personal grooming to conduct to overall demeanor. Unlike loyalty and trustworthiness, professionalism *can* be judged before a potential employer ever meets you. Most interviewers can establish your level of professionalism by your resume and cover letter. Some will even judge the quality of paper on which your resume is printed. We have never actually met a person who lost a job over a watermark being turned the wrong way on a cover letter, but it certainly says something about your professionalism to many who will interview you.

Professionalism is best defined by Bob Adams in his book, *The Complete Resume and Job Search Book for College Students* (1999). He says it is the "ability to fit in with others in a given work group, adhering to their standards."

▲ ▲ ▲

CONFIDENCE AND DECISION-MAKING ABILITIES

Many of you will go into an interview and into the workforce with a stigma facing you, especially if you are a member of the so-called Generation X or Y. Many times people have unfairly pegged you. You are being judged because you are a member of a group of people who are seen as slackers and goof-offs. Don't let this get to you, and don't perpetuate the myth. You can prove that you have much to offer and separate yourself from the pack.

There is a difference between being confident and able to make decisions and being cocky. Confidence comes from experience and calculated risk-taking. Employers are looking for people who are not afraid to make hard decisions and who have confidence in their abilities. When you meet with the person interviewing you, move away from saying (and believing) "I'm a teacher," or "I'm an accountant," or "I'm a computer programmer." Instead, move toward talking about your overall qualities. Talk about your general and specific abilities and characteristics.

▲ ▲ ▲

PRIORITY MANAGEMENT SKILLS

Today, maybe more than any other time in human history, we are faced with more and more to do and what seems like less and less time to do it. In Las Vegas, where millions of people visit each year and where the primary industry is hospitality, one major hotel/casino/resort does not tolerate managers working more than 8 or 9 hours a day. The philosophy is this: If you have to work 12 to 15 hours per day, we have misjudged your job and we need to hire another person, *or* you don't know how to manage your tasks. Believe us when we tell you, these long hours are *not* the norm.

Your success will depend on how well you manage your priorities both personally and professionally. Priority management involves not only getting today's work accomplished but also your ability to plan for the future. You will want to contribute all you can to your career and employer, and you also will want to take time to enjoy your life, your family, your friends, and your relationships. In Chapter 15 we discuss balance and harmony in one's life.

▲ ▲ ▲

THE ABILITY TO CHANGE AND GROW

Less than 10 years ago, few people, if any, could have ever predicted that there would be full-time, well-paid positions called Web Masters. Now you would be hard-pressed to find a company or industry that does not have a one. This is a good example of how changes in technology drive changes in business, education, and industry.

If you are unable or unwilling to change and grow, thousands of your peers can, and will. Our advice is to keep abreast of trends and technology pertaining to your field: Attend conferences, read professional literature, take classes, and have open discussions with colleagues and mentors about the issues surrounding your company and industry.

▲ ▲ ▲

COMPUTER LITERACY

In interviewing three candidates for an Administrative Aide position at my college, one of the basic conditions of employment we set forth for this position was the ability to create and maintain a Web page. When we asked each candidate about their computer skills, two admitted that they had not used a computer in years and one said she could do only D-base. Needless to say, the position went to the person who understood computers, the Internet, basic programming, word processing, spreadsheets, and creating databases. The ability to keep pace with the changes in computer technology may frighten you, yet it is essential to your success. You should make every effort to learn as much as you possibly can about the systems in your office and those on the horizon for your industry.

▲ ▲ ▲

CRITICAL THINKING SKILLS

Not only do employers want employees who can make decisions and proceed with confidence but they also require that you be able to think your way through problems and challenges. Employers are looking for people who can distinguish fact from opinion, identify fallacies, analyze and synthesize information, determine the value of a piece of information, think beyond the obvious, see things from varying angles, and arrive at sound solutions.

▲ ▲ ▲

MULTI-TASKING

A newspaper cartoon suggested that you are too busy if you multi-task in the shower. This may be true, but to keep pace with today's workforce, multi-tasking—the ability to do more than one thing at a time and to do all the tasks well—is essential. If you have not had much experience in multi-tasking, we suggest that you start slowly. Don't take on too many things at one time. As you understand more about working on and completing several tasks at a time, you can expand your abilities in multi-tasking.

▲ ▲ ▲

HUMAN RELATIONSHIP SKILLS

We saved this one for last—certainly not because it is least important but, instead, because this quality is an overriding characteristic of the others.

Employers are looking for people with "people skills." This concept goes much farther than being a team player; it goes to the heart of many workplaces. It touches on your most basic nature. It draws from your most inner self.

The ability to get along with grouchy, cranky, mean, disagreeable, burned-out colleagues is, indeed, a rare quality. But some people do this, and do it well. Peak performers—those at the top of their game—have learned that this world is made up of many types of people and there is never going to be a time devoid of those cranky, grumpy people.

Strive to learn something from everyone, especially people who are hardest to be around. Maybe the only lesson you learn is that you don't want to end up like them. What more valuable lesson could there be?

Knowing Yourself

As you begin your journey, you will start to discover that one of the daily challenges is to have personal and professional lives that are parallel. Quite simply, is there a match between your personal value and goal system and that of your employer and company? Often, people find themselves in a juxtaposition between the two. Will you go against what you value for a hefty raise? Will you relinquish your own goals and dreams for the sake of advancement in a company?

These are questions and challenges that you will face in the years to come. Our advice is to determine who you are, establish the things for which you stand, develop an overriding, ongoing philosophy of life and then, you will be in a better position to make judgments about your future.

References

Adams, B. (1999). *The Complete Resume and Job Search Book for College Students*. Holbrook, MA: Adams Media.

Bolles, R. (1994, 1999). *What Color Is Your Parachute?* Berkley, CA: Ten Speed Press.

CAPSTONES

FOR MAKING THE TRANSITION

The workplace is a vibrant, changing entity.

▲

Writing, speaking, and listening skills are essential to success.

▲

Employers are seeking people with a strong work ethic.

▲

The ability to do more than one task at a time is helpful.

▲

Success involves keeping current with trends and technology.

▲

Loyalty, teamwork, and professionalism are hallmarks in today's workplace.

▲

Employers want to see that you are capable of making decisions and thinking critically.

▲

The ability to work with people from varying walks of life is of utmost importance.

2
CHAPTER

The Job Search Plan

The resume gets your foot in the door; the interview gets the job—but job search comes before everything else. If you match your interests and qualifications to a few select positions, write a good resume, and prepare for an interview, you will usually have success.

PAT MOODY

The first thing you need to know about searching for a job is this: Getting a job—the right job—is hard work! If you are a first-semester senior, now is the time to begin your job search. If you are a second-semester senior, your job search should be one of your top priorities.

By now, you have selected a major that should at least relate to your career interests, although this is not always the case. Many people graduate from college having no idea what they want to do, or they want to do something for which they are ill prepared. Some seniors have chosen majors that are not career-focused, making the job search more difficult. Some majors are challenging and interesting but do not prepare graduates for careers that afford the lifestyle they want. Thus, in some cases, seniors find that the best solution for them is to go to graduate school and prepare for a profession, ideally one that incorporates what they learned as an undergraduate.

For example, if you are a history major, do not want to teach, and have not been able to zero-in on a job that matches your background, you might want to consider law school or a degree in Public Administration. Sometimes the job search demonstrates to students the real need to continue going to school.

Other students have known for a long time exactly what they want to do for the rest of their lives. They know they want to teach or to be an accountant or to become a doctor. Chances are that they have followed a professional career track that enables them to move immediately into the job of their choice.

Still others have pursued professional degrees that have prepared them well for a job but the field is broad, making the job search more complicated. For example, you may have majored in Computer Science. Almost every business needs Computer Science majors, so your task is to narrow the opportunities to a business in which you are interested. You may have majored in Hospitality Management. Now you have to decide if you are interested in a career in the hotel business, the restaurant business, or a tourism-related field.

As you can see, the job search is an individual matter, and it has to be given serious thought. Again, getting the right job is hard work. The time to start is now! To assist you in developing your job search plan and eventually finding the job and career that suites you, this chapter will discuss the following:

▲ Examining your interests

▲ Evaluating your qualifications

▲ Focusing your employer search

▲ Developing the job/career search plan

career centers

internships

employment agencies

newspapers and classifieds

professional journals

companies

guest speakers

professors

professional headhunters

networking

the Internet

Examining Your Interests

What do you want to do? Where do you want to live? What kind of organization appeals to you? Because getting a job usually takes a great deal of time and energy, you want to get the right job the first time if possible. Have you identified your interests? Do you like to work with people, or do you prefer numbers and data? Are salary and benefits the prime factors driving your choice? Do you mind relocating and continuing to relocate? Do you want to travel, or are you a homebody? Do you need the company of colleagues, or do you work best with a computer and modem at home? Before you start the search and draft your resume, hone in on your interests and try to match your job with what you love.

A thorough career search includes the following components:

- Developing a career objective. If you cannot write an objective, you are not ready to begin the search process for a specific job. First, you must read and explore until you have narrowed your focus.
- Writing an effective resume or assembling an outstanding portfolio.
- Developing good interviewing skills.
- Researching organizations to learn more about them, as well as to determine realistic expectations for your employment there.

Evaluating Your Qualifications

Employers want to know what you have to offer them. What are your assets, your strengths and weaknesses, your work experience? Have you managed other people? What have you learned from extracurricular activities and part-time jobs? Do you write well? Are you skilled in using computers? Do you speak a language fluently? If you have never worked, your top priority should be to get a part-time job before you graduate, preferably in the field in which you want to get a job.

Once you have evaluated your interests and your qualifications, you can write your resume and assemble your portfolio (discussed in Chapter 3). While you are writing your resume, you also need to be narrowing the list of companies and positions to which you want to apply.

Have some business cards printed, or print them yourself. Most stationery and copy companies have basic cards you can use to make your own. Choose a card style that is professional and classic. Avoid colorful, flashy cards, especially when you are looking for a job. Professional-looking business cards will make you look better to a potential employer.

Focusing Your Employer Search

Once you have defined what you want to do and have evaluated your qualifications realistically, you need to narrow your search to companies at the top of your list. You need to consider three areas:

1. **Geographic location.** Do you want to be in the South? The Southwest? Are you unwilling to work anywhere except Atlanta or New York or San Francisco? Are you unwilling to relocate when the company wants you to, to get a promotion? Is change difficult for you? You should be realistic about geographic location *before* you take the job. If you accept a job in Denver because you have always lived there and the company wants to transfer you to Connecticut after a year, can you deal with this? If you take a job knowing that it is not going to offer what you want in the long range, you are just prolonging the job search.

2. **Organization focus.** Do you want to work in banking? Textile manufacturing? Real estate? Pharmaceutical sales? Or do you just want a job? You need to narrow the search to organizations that match your interests and qualifications so you don't waste your time.

3. **Job focus.** Can you narrow your job focus to something like this: I want to work as a computer programmer for a software development company in Birmingham, Alabama. I want to work for a publishing company in New York City and begin as an editorial assistant. I want to work as an assistant buyer for a major retailer in the Northwest, preferably Seattle. The more narrow you can define your focus, the easier it is to plan your search.

Developing the Job/Career Search

The first thing you need to know is that a college degree doesn't guarantee you a job. Nevertheless, an excellent grade-point average accompanied by a solid work history and demonstrated leadership skills will make you more desirable as a candidate. If you don't have these qualifications, you may have to work harder, but you can be successful if you start early and persist. You will discover that employers may use the open or the hidden market to recruit employees.

THE OPEN MARKET

CAREER CENTER. One of the best places for college students to find a job is usually through the career center on campus. Not only does this center help with resume writing and interviewing skills but it typically schedules Career Fairs during the early fall and spring. It is much easier to get an interview with recruiters who are looking for students to hire than it is to respond to newspaper ads. The recruiters come to your campus, and all you have to do is to get an interview and prepare. Another good thing about on-campus interviewing is that you are competing only with other students. In most other situations you will be competing with experienced workers.

You also might check the bulletin board in career centers for job postings. Another source of jobs may be a bulletin board in your department's office. If you apply for one of these jobs, write a cover letter and a resume targeted to that specific job. Call the company and get a person's name to whom you can address your letter. Blind letters are less likely to prompt a response.

INTERNSHIPS OR COOPERATIVE WORK EXPERIENCES. If your college offers an internship or a cooperative work experience, you may want to explore this possibility as a career opportunity. If you work for a company as an intern and perform well on the job, you most likely will be offered a permanent position. If you take an internship, you should do your very best work even if you decide, after being on the job for a while, that this is not for you. You need references, and the best ones are supervisors for whom you have worked and performed well.

EMPLOYMENT AGENCIES. Often, companies work with employment agencies because these agencies screen applicants and send the companies only the top candidates. You should leave your resume with reputable companies. Ask them for references and don't sign anything with an employment agency unless you read it carefully. You might be agreeing to give the firm several months of your salary in exchange for their locating a job for you. Be sure to ask the agent if the employment fee is paid by the company that has placed the job with the agency.

NEWSPAPERS AND CLASSIFIED ADS. Classified ads in newspapers can be a good source for part of your job search, but you should not limit your search to newspaper ads. The competition usually is much tougher, and many of the best jobs are not placed in the newspaper. By all means, though, include this source as one of your targets.

PROFESSIONAL JOURNALS. You can find professional journals in your library. Professors are another source to get names of appropriate journals. Many professional organizations offer

ΛDVIᏟᏃ FROM Λ MᏃNTOR

Lucinda Moyano,

Assistant Attorney General
State of Oregon, Salem

One of the most important aspects of my profession is that of relationships with other people. I think that relationships can be viewed in two ways, internal and external. In my agency, we have a very collegial office where we work well together. I think that this is very important for the success of the office and the success of our clients. I also think that this is important because we value each others' opinions, respect each other, and depend on each other. My relationships at work are important because they help me establish networks for future growth.

Externally, relationships are just as important. If you are in a very unproductive or adversarial relationship with another lawyer or agency,

 this would be counterproductive to your client. Because of the poor relationship, you, your agency, or your client may suffer. Adversarial relationships can also come back to haunt you as you think about moving from one job or profession to another. You will quickly find that Disney has it right: "It's a small world after all."

student memberships at a greatly reduced price. These memberships give you a professional organization to put on your resume and also provide potential job opportunities.

PROFESSIONAL HEADHUNTERS. Although professional headhunters typically seek out people with proven experience, in some cases they are interested in new graduates. It depends on your background and qualifications. If you are a physical therapist, for example, and there is a shortage in this field, they may contact you. Even though this is a long shot in some fields, it is worth a try, included with other sources in your job search. Certainly you need to remember this job search source as you gain more experience and want to change jobs.

DEVELOPING YOUR OWN NETWORK. You should develop a network of people you know who may work for a company in which you have an interest. People on the "inside" have an advantage in helping you get your foot in the door. What about your dad's golf partner? A friend of your mom's? What about a friend who is a graduate, knows your work style, and is working for a company in which you have an interest?

- **Contact professors in your major field.** They are excellent sources to be included in your network. If you have excelled in a professor's class, he or she may be willing to help you. On the other hand,

ΛDVIᏨΣ
CONTINUED.
One of the things that I learned in college was the importance of positive relationships and developing communication and interpersonal skills. The interpersonal skills that I learned have helped me advance in my career. I learned early that if you can't get along with people, you're going to have a very hard time in this world.

In the office of the Assistant Attorney General, it would be very hard to learn from other people or share ideas with other people if we did not have relationships that promote open, honest communication and interpersonal skills. I think that we must learn to be open to others. Externally, if you have good interpersonal skills and know how to communicate, you may be able to work out a problem for your client much more easily than if you do not possess these skills. If you're a jerk, it may be harder to get things done.

As you enter the world of work, remember that everyone you meet can be, and very well may be, a potential employer or reference. Nurture those relationships, and you will reap the benefits.

if you have constantly cut class or showed up late, you probably cannot count on a professor to recommend you. Professors believe their credibility is on the line when they recommend someone to associates in their profession.

• **Contact companies in which you are interested** even if they have not advertised an open position. Write an unsolicited letter, include your resume, and follow up with a phone call. Many times this results in very little, but sometimes a resume can hit their office at just the right time. Don't be too discouraged if you get a lot of form letters or no response at all. Some companies get many more letters of application than they can review.

• **Show an interest in guest speakers** if they visit your classes. Stay afterward and ask questions. On the days you have speakers, give your grooming extra care. Although you may not want to wear a suit, you shouldn't wear sweatpants either. Give the speaker a business card and express an interest in talking to his or her company. These people usually want to help students or they would not have showed up to speak. Many of them have good contacts and may be helpful to you even if you are not interested in their company.

The Best New Search Tool Available—The Internet

The Internet has changed the rules of almost everything, job search plans included. You now can sit at your computer and research companies with which you have an interview, and you *must* research before an interview. You can expect to be asked this question: "What do you know about XYZ Company?" If you reply, "Nothing," you have blown the interview.

You also can search for jobs on the Internet because many large companies are now posting job openings. In turn, you can post your resume on the Internet. If you are planning to go to graduate school, you may find an assistantship via the Internet. The Internet is a rich source of career information—and it is at your fingertips!

PLACES TO LOOK

As you explore the Internet, you will find thousands of jobs listed all over the world. In this space we cannot list all the possibilities, but some of the major sources are listed below. In addition, the references at the end of this chapter may be useful to you.

BBS (bulletin board services)

news.announce.newusers

bionet.jobs (large list of jobs in biological sciences)

uk.jobs.d (jobs listed in the United Kingdom)

balt.jobs (jobs listed in the Baltimore/Washington, DC area)

us.jobs.offered (jobs listed in the United States)

JOBS SPECIFICALLY FOR COLLEGE STUDENTS

misc.jobs.offered.entry

telnet college.career.com

gopher chronicle.merit.edu (jobs listed in education)

American Mathematical Society (math jobs)

OCC (Online Career Center)

> Try **occ.com** or **www.occ.com/occ/**

> Send your resume to Online Career Center via email to **occ-resumes@occ.com** or you can mail your resume to:

> > Online Resume Service
> > 1713 Hemlock Lane
> > Plainfield, IN 46168–1830

CareerWeb

web.cweb.com/

Jobplace

news.jobweb.org/cgi-bin/lwgate/jobplace

The Monster Board

www.monster.com/

These sites are just a few that are available, but they will get you started on your search. For tips on how to list your resume on the web, refer to Chapter 3.

References

Dixon, Pam. (1998). *Be Your Own Headhunter Online: Get the Job You Want by Using the Information Superhighway.* New York: Random House.

Glossbrenner, Alfred and Emily. (1995). *Finding a Job on the Internet.* New York: McGraw-Hill.

Jandt, Fred E., and Nemnich, Mary B. (1995). *Using the Internet in Your Job Search.* Indianapolis: JIST Works.

Kennedy, Joyce L. (1995). *Hook Up, Get Hired! The Internet Job Search Revolution.* New York: John Wiley.

CAPSTONES
FOR DEVELOPING A JOB SEARCH PLAN

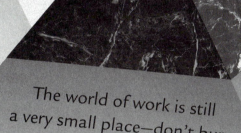

The world of work is still a very small place—don't burn bridges.

▲

Job-seekers must know what their interests and skills are. What do you have to offer?

▲

Job aspirants have to know their qualifications.

▲

Job-seekers should know *how* they want to work.

▲

Job-seekers should know *where* they want to work.

▲

A variety of resources can aid in your search: your college Career Center, internships, guest speakers, people with whom you have networked, professional journals, and employment agencies.

▲

The Internet can help in your search for employment.

The Resume and Career Portfolio

Most people fail to get the job they really want, fail not because they are not qualified but because they failed in the interview. And most failure occurs in the interview because they aren't prepared.

DAVID W. CRAWLEY, JR.

The most important part of the job search process is the preparation that must be done prior to the interview. Two key elements of this preparation are your resume and your career portfolio. Your resume is a key component in your career search. A carefully crafted resume communicates your past history (skills and experience) that makes you the ideal candidate for the position. It is the first marketing piece and in many cases must stand alone when a recruiter is determining whether to interview you.

Just as a well-designed resume can be a valuable first step, a poorly designed resume can doom you to failure before you ever leave your house. There is not a single way to develop your career resume and format, as they vary from discipline to discipline. What this chapter does is outline the key components of resumes, with a discussion of how to develop a resume that will represent your best efforts.

The second sales tool is your career portfolio. A career portfolio is basically an expansion of your resume. "The theory behind portfolios evolves from a Deweyan idea that learning involves an experiential continuum in which new knowledge is built upon and mediated by prior knowledge and values. In portfolios, conscious reflection on one's experiences serves as a vehicle of professional development" (Lyons, 1998).

As more and more recruiters turn to behavior-based interviews, students need to have concrete visual documentation of their work that extends beyond a resume. In this chapter you will:

▲ Review the various types of resumes.

▲ Learn how to develop your personal resume.

▲ Learn how to create sample cover letters.

▲ Learn how to solicit letters of reference.

▲ Learn how to write acceptance and rejection letters.

▲ Understand what a career portfolio is, why you need it, and how to develop one.

▲ Determine what experiences you have that the career portfolio should include.

Different Types of Resumes

The different types of resumes can be classified into the following formats:

- *Chronological resume:* organizes education and work experience in a sequential manner.
- *Functional resume:* organizes your work and experience around specific skills and duties.
- *Combination resume:* combines elements of the chronological format with the functional format.
- *Narrative resume:* provides a discussion that expands information in the major categories of the resume.
- *Teaching resume:* used by experienced teachers; outlines the courses they have taught.
- *Curriculum vitae:* outlines the courses taught and includes a bibliography of articles and books published.

Most graduating seniors choose one of the first three types—chronological, functional, or combination.

Developing Your Personal Resume

When choosing the format for your personal resume, you need to take into careful consideration the field in which you wish to be employed, as well as the company with which you are interviewing. The "one-size-fits-all" ideology does not work with resumes. You can use the computer to customize your resume to meet the needs of individual employers.

As you design your personal resume, keep in mind the types of employers with which you anticipate interviewing. Generally they will fit into a couple of broad categories, necessitating only a couple of different resumes.

As you begin to develop your resume, allow yourself plenty of time to develop it. Enlist several qualified proofreaders to check your work. We cannot stress strongly enough the need for your resume to be perfect. A simple typographical error or misuse of grammar can disqualify you from the job of your dreams. Don't allow a lack of attention to detail to stand between you and your future career.

Designing a Cover Letter that Works

Whenever you send your resume to a company, whether it is in response to a posted advertisement or requested from you, you must send a cover letter with it. Most recruiters will tell you that they read four times as many cover letters as they do resumes because, if the cover letter does not "strike a cord," they don't look past it to the resume.

Writing a cover letter is almost as dreaded as writing a resume. For this reason, many applicants make the mistake of using a "canned" cover letter to accompany all of their resumes. Using the same cover letter regardless of the situation is the quickest way to ensure that your resume will not be considered.

Both your resume and cover letter should be typed and printed on a fine-quality paper. Cheap paper and poor-quality printing sends the message that you don't care. This is not the place to pinch pennies. Buy a good-quality paper stock, and make sure that the print quality is excellent.

A good cover letter should be personally addressed and job-specific. This letter is probably competing with those of several, if not hundreds, of other people seeking the same job. Therefore, your letter is the first step in separating you from the pack. If possible, address your letter to a specific person. At all costs, avoid the dreaded "Dear sir or madam" or "To whom it may concern." In most cases, a phone call to the company will yield the name of the person, his or her title, and the address. Always verify spellings, even with common names.

Once your letter is addressed correctly, the first paragraph should answer the question, "Why am I writing?" If your resume has been requested, be sure to indicate this in the letter. If the letter is to someone other than the individual who requested your resume, make sure to include the name of the person who requested your resume. If you are responding to an advertisement, include the name of the newspaper and the date of the advertisement.

The second paragraph should state clearly why you are qualified for the position you are seeking. Use your cover letter to highlight the areas of your experience that specifically qualify you for the job. If you have a difficult time articulating why you are uniquely qualified for the job, perhaps you should not be applying for the position. Your cover letter is not the place to list all of your qualifications but, rather, to indicate the two or three qualities that best qualify you for the position. You also may include specific qualifications that are not on your resume.

Your final paragraph should address the question, "Where do we go from here?" Do not be ambiguous by saying something trite such as, "I hope to hear from you in the near future" or, "If you have any questions, please do not hesitate to call me." Be proactive by stating that you will be following up with a phone call to discuss your resume in more detail.

Once you have said you are going to call, you must actually do it. During this call, ask for an appointment to discuss the company with them—not the job you are applying for, but the company.

Prior to your meeting, do extensive research on the company and, if possible, on the person with whom you will be interviewing. Be prepared with specific questions about the company. If there is a match between you and the company, discussion about the position will flow naturally from there.

Soliciting Letters of Reference

Five steps are involved in soliciting letters of reference.

Step 1: Select three to five people to serve as references. In determining whom to select, choose people who are familiar with your work ability. Current and former employers with whom you have had a good working relationship are excellent reference sources. College professors are another excellent source.

If you do not know anyone who falls into these two categories, consider asking friends of your family who are respected members of the community.

As you consider possible reference sources, choose individuals who are responsible and timely in their reply. References are a reflection of you, and if they do not respond appropriately, they will cast a shadow on your credibility.

Step 2: Request permission from your reference sources to use them as such. During your conversation with them, discuss your career goals and aspirations. Give them a copy of your resume and cover letter. Ask them to critique these for you and offer suggestions for changes.

Step 3: Obtain all necessary contact information from your references: name, job title, business address, email address, phone number, and fax number.

Step 4: Send thank-you letters to people who agree to serve as references for you. Stay in contact with them throughout your job search, giving them updates and periodic thank-yous in the form of cards, emails, or phone calls. At the end of your job search, a small token of your appreciation is also appropriate.

Step 5: Develop a typed list of all references, including contact information. Carry this with you to all interviews.

The Career Portfolio

The career portfolio is a professionally assembled binder containing:

- statement of originality and confidentiality
- career goals
- resume
- skill areas
- certifications, diplomas
- degrees and awards
- academic specializations or concentrations
- professional memberships
- community service activities
- biographies of individuals on your reference list.

ΛDVIƆƐ FROM Λ MƐNTOR

Garcia Tate,

Professor, College of Applied Professional Science
University of South Carolina, Columbia

Good written communication skills are necessary for success in any business or organization. Your resume and career portfolio are written documents used to enhance your job search and future career. As a college student, you are required to attend classes, listen intently, organize lecture materials, and convert that information into meaningful text for future use. These same skills are applicable in developing your career portfolio. Gather materials and then translate them into a meaningful document that chronicles your professional career.

The statement of originality and confidentiality basically declares that the work contained in your portfolio represents your work. If you are

The skills you develop as you work on your career-search documents

are skills that you will continue to use throughout your professional career. Today, I am a university professor and I'm still using the skills I developed in college and throughout my early career development. Not only must I keep accurate notes of my career progress for tenure and promotion within the institution, but if I ever plan to move to a new university, these documents will serve including work done in group projects, you should include the names of all of the individuals with whom you worked as well as your percentage of contribution. If you are doing campus interviewing, the recruiter might interview your co-authors, so you want this statement to avoid any misunderstanding. The statement also should ensure that the recruiter understands that this work should not be copied without your permission.

Although many people believe that career goals should be stated in a resume, we disagree. We believe that career goals on a resume are trite and used only by new graduates. A better place for your career goals is in your portfolio. Here you are able to provide a more comprehensive overview of your goals. These goals should address all work-related areas that encompass not only the position you would like to attain but also the skills you would like to acquire, the professional organizations in which you would like to participate, and any volunteer work with which you would like to get involved.

You also should include an overview of your personal and professional development goals. These goals may or may not be directly related to your work. They should show that you are a well-rounded individual who intends to maintain a balance in your life.

The skills portion of this portfolio should include a detailed overview of your experience and skills in specific job-related areas. For example, you should include an overview of your computer skills, skills associated with the functional areas of management (marketing, accounting, finance, human resource management, lodging, culinary management, and so on).

You also should include examples of work you have completed that provide testimony of your experience in these areas. This is an excellent place to include copies of papers you have written, class projects you have completed, projects at work for which you have a primary role in implement-

ΛDVIζΣ
CONTINUED.

me well in my career portfolio. As technology advances, so does your ability to develop a "first-rate" resume and career portfolio. Take advantage of the new desktop publishing programs available to you, as well as color scanners and color copiers to make your career portfolio a professional document you can be proud of.

Always remember though, that style does not make up for substance. Your writing skills must be outstanding. The experiences documented in your career portfolio also must be meaningful and life/career-enhancing. While preparing these documents take the time to reflect on your accomplishments and to distinguish areas that may need more attention. These documents are excellent barometers of your career growth.

ing or managing, and the like. If you, like many of your fellow classmates, neglected to keep copies, include letters of recommendation that document your competency in the areas you list.

Your portfolio also should include copies of certifications, diplomas, degrees earned, and any special awards and recognitions you have received. A copy of your transcript should be included in this section. The transcript certifies your plan of study and your specialization within content areas. This section allows the recruiter to peruse your accomplishments without your having to brag about yourself.

Another part of your portfolio involves listing professional memberships you hold, as well as copies of membership cards, citations you've received, letters of recommendation regarding your participation in these organizations, and so on. In today's world, companies are interested in hiring a balanced, well-rounded individual. For this reason, we suggest that you include your community-service activities, which confirms your commitment to the world outside of your own little sector. These may be, for example, philanthropic activities of student and professional organizations of which you are a member and community projects through your place of worship.

Portfolios give testimony to accomplishments through a concrete, visual product. The portfolio serves to document the resume. In a resume, you provide a thumbnail sketch of your accomplishments. In a portfolio, you coin an old phrase: "Put your money where your mouth is."

The presentation of a portfolio should be carefully timed. It is not appropriate to walk into an interview and immediately whip out your portfolio for the recruiter. As the interview unfolds and the recruiter asks you specific questions regarding areas of your resume, you may use your portfolio to document your answers. The portfolio you develop during your college years can continue to be valuable in future employment. Therefore, you should continuously update and change this portfolio with projects and accomplishments during your career. This portfolio will serve you well when you are being considered for a promotion or a move to another company. Although the portfolio ideally is started at the beginning of your college career, it is not too late to put together an outstanding portfolio.

The Nuts and Bolts of Creating Your Career Portfolio

Organization of material is important in career development. If you have not already developed a system for maintaining career related documents, we suggest the following method.

1. Purchase a file box or designate a drawer in your filing cabinet for only career-related documents. We prefer the file box because it is less likely to be used as an overflow drawer for noncareer-related information. Hanging file folders should be labeled in this way:
   a. Resume
   b. Skills
   c. Work Samples
   d. Reference Letters
   e. Certifications, Awards, Degrees, and Diplomas
   f. Academic Plan of Study
   g. Work in Progress
   h. Professional Organizations
   i. Community Service

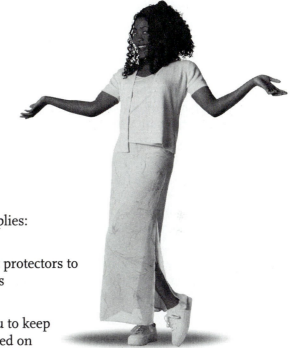

2. Include in your box the following supplies:
   a. Computer disk holder
   b. Clear plastic 3-hole-punched sheet protectors to hold documents and work samples
   c. Labels for your projects
   d. Plastic photo holders to enable you to keep pictures of projects you have worked on
3. Commit to making an extra copy of projects, invitations, awards, and other career-related documents and placing them immediately in the appropriate file folder in your file box.
4. Monthly, commit to spending approximately 1 hour updating your career documents. During this time, you can label your projects, encase them in plastic protectors, and prepare them for your portfolio in whatever way is needed.

If you are diligent in maintaining this system, developing your career portfolio will be an easily accomplished task. This system also will enable you to be prepared for your annual evaluation. We suggest that you be an active participant in your annual evaluation by taking your career portfolio with you so you can visually present your accomplishments for the previous year. We have found that this format greatly increases an individual's ability to build a case for promotions and raises. Chapter 11 provides a further discussion on this topic.

As you begin to assemble your career portfolio, careful attention to detail and an eye for style, creativity, and professionalism are necessary. If you lack these abilities, solicit the help of a friend who has these strengths, buy him or her pizza or whatever, and ask this friend to help you think-through the assembly of your career portfolio. Because this will be seen by career recruiters and your superiors, only the highest quality of materials should be used. Your portfolio should be as professionally done as possible. Never hand-write anything; always use a computer. Never 3-hole punch the actual documents; always place them within page protectors. Your career portfolio is not a scrapbook for cut-and-paste keepsakes. It is an important tool in your career development.

We suggest that you use a leather, zippered, 3-ring binder. If possible, have a brass name plate engraved and installed on the front cover. Use extra-wide 3-ring tabs labeled with the same headings you used in your file box to separate the major sections of your career portfolio. When inserting documents, use either a color scanner or a color copier to make copies of your important documents, then return the originals to your file box. Use labeled sheet protectors to hold the individual documents. For example, within your resume section, the resume would be encased in a plastic sheet protector labeled "Resume."

A carefully assembled career portfolio is an important part of career management and should not be limited to the job search. This document will not only enhance your marketability but also provide you with a cohesive history of this part of your life.

Creating Acceptance and Rejection Letters

The resume and cover letter are important in creating a positive first impression, but they should not overshadow the importance of your letters of acceptance and rejection. The acceptance letter may or may not be your first written correspondence with your immediate superior. In any case, it should command special attention. Likewise, if you are rejecting an offer, you should be mindful of the old saying, "Never burn bridges" and carefully word the letter of rejection so as not to offend the recipient. You never know when this individual will play an important role in your career in the future.

Both types of letters must be specific, and there is no reason for the letters to be lengthy. They should be addressed to the appropriate individual with copies to secondary people and should clearly outline your decision. You should thank the addressees for their time and state how excited you are to become a part of their team (in the case of the acceptance letter) or wish them well for the future if the letter is one of rejection.

References

Lyons, N. (1998). *With Portfolio in Hand: Validating the New Teacher Professionalism.* New York: Columbia University, Teachers College Press.

Swanson, D. (1998). *The Resume Solution.* Indianapolis: JIST Works.

Williams, A. G., and Hall, K. (1997). *Creating Your Career Portfolio.* Upper Saddle River, NJ: Prentice Hall.

CAPSTONES

FOR PREPARING YOUR RESUME AND PORTFOLIO

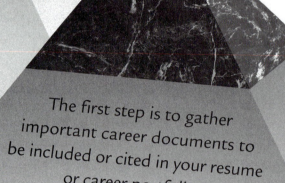

The first step is to gather important career documents to be included or cited in your resume or career portfolio.

▲

Time should be spent weekly working on both your resume and career portfolio.

▲

The help and wisdom of respected friends, professors, and others are valuable in reviewing these documents and providing insight.

▲

When developing any of these tools, only the best quality of supplies will do.

▲

The quality of every facet of your career search and the documents you develop will impact your entire career.

CHAPTER 4

Professional Presence

Professionals who master business etiquette become more favored in the workplace.

ANN C. HUMPHRIES

Several years ago, John Malloy, an "image guru," made this statement: "As much as one-third of your success depends on what you wear." In Malloy's opinion, your appearance, image, and presence contribute greatly to your overall success in your career.

Sometimes people get presence mixed up with posture. Posture is what your mother told you about all the time: "Stand up straight." "Don't let your shoulders slump." Presence is that certain something that sets you apart from most other people. Presence is how you enter a room, how you walk, how you shake hands, how you dress, how you speak, how much confidence and energy you demonstrate, how outgoing you are. You probably have seen some people who make others' heads turn, and not necessarily because they are extraordinarily handsome or beautiful. Many times it's confidence, coupled with extraordinary grooming or clothing and a sparkling personality.

Some of you reading this book will say, "But I can't do these things. I'm very shy. I don't like to bring attention to myself." The answer is to "fake it until you make it." Most people consider themselves shy, yet most manage to cover it up. You are going to get attention. It's just a matter of whether the attention is positive or negative. Your image should match your ambitions. If you were going to work today, would your wardrobe reflect your ambitions? Would you look chic and stylish or would you appear frumpy and nondescript? Would you look like a student or like a businessperson? Do you want to look businesslike or sexy? What would people say about your grooming? What does your body language say about you? Image is a complete package and anyone can improve greatly. Some people are naturally more attractive than others, and some are more graceful and charming, but anyone can learn to develop presence and build a better image.

To assist you with your professional image and presence, this chapter will address the following topics:

▲ Inner change

▲ Developing a sense of what is best for you as a female or a male

▲ Attending business meetings

▲ What is "business casual?"

▲ Attending the company party

▲ Working and networking a room

▲ Dining etiquette

nner Change

To build the right image and develop presence, you may need to start with changing how you feel about yourself. Often, body language reflects how someone really feels about himself or herself on the inside. You might be saying all the right things, but if your words don't come together with your expressions and your tone of voice, prospective employers will not believe you. You cannot be convincing if you slump, drag around, or fail to make eye contact. Your body language speaks volumes about you.

Observe your body language in a mirror. Are you surprised at some of the messages you are sending out? Did anyone call you names when you were growing up? Did you have critical parents? Did a teacher embarrass you and make you self- conscious? Are you critical of yourself and make negative comments about yourself? The first step toward building a positive presence is to learn to love yourself and to believe that you really are okay. Although some people need counseling to overcome childhood traumas, most of us can help ourselves simply by saying positive things to ourselves, by setting physical goals and achieving them, and by associating with people who make us feel good. As you work on your exterior, work on your interior every day.

One exercise that works if you do it often enough is to write down all the good things you can think of about yourself every day. Keep doing this until you can name 15 good things in a minute. Look at this list each morning and each night before you go to bed. Add good things to the list daily. By doing this, you are programming your brain to focus on the positive things about you. When you program your brain, your body will carry out the positive message.

Visualize yourself looking the way you want to look. Picture yourself in a great-looking business suit walking into a room with confidence and shaking hands with important people. Several times a day, visualize what you want to become. Under no circumstances should you say negative things about yourself to yourself or to other people. Certainly, you don't want to boast or exaggerate about yourself, but you absolutely must not talk down about yourself. If you have a habit of doing this, make up your mind now to stop it. Listen to what you are saying about you. Do you invite negative feelings?

You may have to move away from a certain group of people or individuals with whom you have been associating. If some of your friends aren't as ambitious as you are or if they engage in things you don't want to participate in, you might need to gradually move away from bad influences and spend more time with people who challenge you and lift you up.

Sometimes you can really love someone who is toxic to you. Examine all your relationships as you get ready to build the new and exciting person you can become. You are about to enter a new world where no one knows your past. Invent who you want to become and start building that person in your mind and in your actions.

Developing a Sense of What Is Best for You

▲ ▲ ▲

WOMEN

Maybe your roommate wears bright colors and has bleached blonde hair. Because she is popular with men, you have tried to emulate her style, but you have not felt comfortable in doing so. You have to do what is right for you.

As a businesswoman, you want to look the part. You don't necessarily want to wear clothes that make you stand out; rather, you want to look good so that people will respond to you appropriately. If you stand out, you have to be sure it is for the right reasons. You need to wear classic business suits in dark colors, stylish but reasonable high-heeled shoes, and real gold or silver jewelry. Purses and belts preferably are leather. Your blouses should be tailored; you should avoid fussy prints, frilly lace, and sexy garments. Likewise, you should avoid pastel colors, especially pink (which screams "baby girl") and bright, garish colors. If you wear sleeveless dresses of big floral prints, you might consider more appropriate attire! You need to learn to see yourself as attractive, classy, and successful.

Although wearing pants is acceptable in most businesses, women should stick to pantsuits that have matching blazer and pants. The pants should be hemmed at the proper length, whatever is stylish but never too short! Sleeves should be hemmed so they do not extend below the wrist. Most clothes require some alterations.

Business dresses or nice pantsuits are fine on most workdays, but if you have a very important meeting, wear a suit with a matching skirt. The best colors for business are navy blue, gray, black, burgundy, charcoal, olive, tan, and khaki. Avoid shocking bright colors and large prints. Pinstripes are too masculine, as are some other patterns. You want to look feminine but tailored and classic. Women have too much going for them today to try to look like men.

Your supervisor should not have to tell you that your pants are too tight, your sweater too sexy, or your blouse too sheer. Use good sense. At work, you want to be known for your business acumen, not your sex appeal. You must make up your mind early in the game to be taken seriously at work or you will not be. Once you have lost that image, it is difficult to get it back.

Your hair should be well-groomed, clean, and shiny. Avoid excessively long hair. On the other hand, you don't want a haircut that is so short it looks like a man's. You should avoid extremes that call attention to you for all the wrong reasons.

We hope you have not been wearing rings in your eyelids, studs in your tongue, 10 earrings in each ear, and rings on every finger. If you have, they've got to go. The business world does not look kindly at out-of-step dress and appearance. First of all, you won't get a job. Second, you won't be taken seriously at work. Observe what the upper-level women wear; find one whose clothing and jewelry you admire, and emulate that person. You will not find a woman executive with 14 earrings placed all around her ears, nor will she have a stud in her tongue or a tattoo in a visible place.

Take good care of your nails and avoid bright nail polish. Your makeup should be conservative and neat. Your jewelry should be simple—one ring on each hand unless it is your wedding and engagement rings. A nice, simple gold watch and one bracelet is enough at work. Hose should coordinate with your outfit, but usually a suntan color or a barely black color works for most business occasions. Avoid patterned hose, colored hose, and white hose.

MEN

One of the best ways for men to stand out is by dressing in an outstanding manner. The average male does not give a great deal of attention to his appearance, so when a man does it right, he gets a lot of attention. Women have many more choices than men—and many more ways of making bad decisions. Any man who wants to become a sharp dresser can do so if he is willing to work at it.

The best times for men to buy suits are after Christmas and after the Fourth of July when most nice men's stores put their suits on sale. You might also look for warehouse sales, which often provide excellent bargains if you know how to shop for them.

Many suits can be worn year around except perhaps on the coldest or hottest days. If you live in the South, you don't need heavy wool clothes because you will get very little wear from them. Regardless of where you live, the fabric in your suits should contain wool because it helps suits keep their shape better after cleaning. If you are taking a traveling position, you need clothes that won't wrinkle badly.

If you are going to work in a company where men wear suits and ties, you need to start building a wardrobe *now*, as many college men own few dress clothes. You need at least two interviewing suits—navy blue and charcoal gray. Once you own these two colors, you can expand your wardrobe.

Other nice additions include a subtle glen plaid and a charcoal gray pinstripe with narrow stripes. If you are in sales, you might want to purchase a khaki or olive suit and wear it with a light blue shirt. Research shows that this combination presents a warm and inviting appearance. You should avoid black because it is an overpowering color. Likewise, avoid pastels and anything that even remotely appears like a wild pattern or color.

If you must interview in a navy blazer and gray pants, be sure they are immaculately pressed and clean. A navy blazer or a nice sport coat with coordinating slacks are fine for normal days at work, but if the occasion is important, you should wear a suit.

You should own at least 10 dress shirts, including several white shirts and at least two light blue shirts. Pinstripes, as well as stylish

ΛDVIᴄƐ FRØM Λ MƐNTØR

Joanna Hibler, President

Southwestern Oklahoma State University, Weatherford, OK

On any given day, I work with regents, alumni, legislators, faculty, staff, and students. Every time I meet with any colleague, alumni, or regent, my professional image is a direct statement on my university. Not only is the way I dress important, but also the way I "carry myself" in meetings, at lunch, or in a casual conversation with a student.

As you enter the world of work, you will quickly realize that those people who have learned the fine art of professional image seem to have the upper edge in many situations. Professional image entails dress, grooming, hygiene, posture, walk, and stance. Basically, your professional image is the visual aspect of who you are and how much you respect yourself.

Professional image does not mean that you have to wear a $2,000 business suit and fine Italian shoes, but it does mean that you show a sense of pride and care in your clothing and grooming. It may be that the dress code in your new place of employment is business-casual. If so, take pride in the casual look you choose for yourself. This choice of image will carry you far.

colored shirts, are a good addition to your wardrobe. For interviewing purposes, there is only one color—white—and it must be starched and immaculate. All dress shirts must have long sleeves, no matter what the temperature. One sure way of advertising that you don't know how to dress is to wear short-sleeved dress shirts. You might as well hang a sign around your neck.

A small monogram in a dark, coordinating color on the left cuff is a nice touch and makes you look more like the upper-level executives. If you feel comfortable doing this, you should have at least one shirt with French cuffs—which means you have to own a pair of cufflinks. By using good shirts and ties, you can stretch a new graduate's wardrobe and make it appear that you have more clothes than you do.

Every man needs a blue blazer with brass buttons. If you are tall and slim, you might choose a double-breasted blazer. If you are short and stocky, you want to avoid this style. Your suits should be either two-button or three-button. Stay away from trendy suits such as four-button that waste your money and make you look like a college boy instead of a businessman. If you button your suit coat, you should button only the top button, never all of them.

You need black and brown shoes and belts. Young men can do okay with tasseled loafers, but lace-up cap-toed shoes are good if you are working in a company where the men dress in an upscale manner. The dressiest shoe a man can wear is the lace-up, wing-tip shoe, but this may seem a little old for new graduates. The cap-toe is more of a young man's shoe. Shoes, of course, must be polished—always—and the heels should not look worn down.

Socks should be black if worn with navy or gray, and they should not show your bare leg if you cross your legs. Actually, to meet standards of good dress, they should go up to the knee. *Never* wear white socks with a business suit. White socks normally are used for athletic events in which you participate or with very casual outfits, but never at work! Patterned socks usually mark a well-dressed man—assuming, of course, that the man knows how to select subdued, sophisticated patterns. Like the rest of your wardrobe, socks should not be loud or wild. Argyles are a no-no!

Your ties should be stylish and bought with careful consideration. If you don't know how to choose a tie, get help at a good men's store. Your mother or your girlfriend may or may not know how to help select ties. The odds are good that they don't. Ties should be silk, of a stylish width, and have no spots on them. Ties should not have the same background as the suit or blazer unless you are dressing in the currently stylish monochromatic color scheme. This style may not be in vogue next year, so if you can't afford many clothes, buy just one of these shirts and ties to wear when you want to look especially nice. Do not wear this style on an interview, though.

Attending Business Meetings

When you enter a room for a business meeting, take a leather portfolio with you. Leave in your office everything else that you don't need for this meeting. Use a pen that looks expensive. Be prepared for the meeting. Because you are new, you should not talk too much. Nothing is worse than a new kid on the block who is a know-it-all. You should, however, try to make one strong, positive statement at every meeting or ask one thought-provoking question. This practice begins to establish you as a solid thinker who comes to meetings prepared.

Business-Casual

Many businesses are beginning to "dress down," especially on Friday. Although you don't want to overdress when others are casual, you don't want to go to great extremes with your casual dress either. Actually, it is just as expensive to dress well for casual occasions as it is to dress for business—and more difficult for some people.

Business-casual for women is a nice pantsuit or a classic, tailored dress. Avoid simple skirts and sweaters, sleeveless blouses—anything that might resemble tee-shirts and sweatpants. You are not likely to see women executives dressing in any of these outfits, so neither should you. You want to be considered part of the up-and-coming young executives, not someone from the clerical pool. Maintain impeccable grooming and style regardless of what everybody else is doing.

On casual days, men should wear a good pair of dress slacks and a golf shirt or a knit shirt with a blazer. You also can wear a button-down-collar shirt with slacks and a blazer. Under no circumstances should you wear tee-shirts and wrinkled khakis or tennis shoes. Some people really mess up with casual dress, and they stand out for all the wrong reasons. Business-casual absolutely does not mean "anything goes." Some employees ruin their chances for advancement by being too careless about their dress and appearance. Again, observe the executives. What do they wear? Emulate them.

You (both men and women) should keep a blazer in your office in case of an emergency that requires you to show some semblance of being dressed in something other than casual. This is another reason you don't ant to go to work looking too casual. What if one of your most important ents calls and says, "I'm coming right over"?

Men should have no earrings, tattoos, beards, goatees, or other distinguishing distractions that set them apart from the upper-level business executives in the company. If you go to work for a computer company, you may see many programmers or technicians dressing in an unorthodox manner. The best advice for you, though, is still to maintain the standard dress at work if you plan to end up in the executive suite.

The Company Party

Don't party at the company party! Arrive a little late and leave a little early. If everyone else is staying very late and drinking too much, this is a good reason for you to excuse yourself and leave—especially women. You should never drink more than one drink at a company function. Nurse that drink as long as you are there, and refrain from drinking simply because the liquor is free. This is not the place for you to have too much to drink and make a fool of yourself.

Wear something that is in good taste. This is a work function—not a social gathering with your best buddies. Women certainly want to look attractive, but not overly sexy. Wives of upper management are not likely to dress in skimpy, tight clothes. You want to fit with them.

If you are attending a swim party, don't swim. You will look like a drowned rat while everyone else is still fresh and attractive. Don't parade around in a swimsuit even if you look like a movie star. Neither men nor women will win friends by insisting on showing off a great body. This is not the place!

If you are playing golf or tennis at a club, you need to know the rules and dress the part. Look like *somebody*. Learning to play golf reasonably well is worth the effort for men and women alike. Many important discussions take place on the golf course. If you are entertaining clients or participating in a company golf outing, take your attire seriously. Executives do pay attention.

Working a Room Like a Pro

As a businessperson, you probably will attend cocktail parties. You should consider them an extension of work. You are there to make contacts, make a good impression, network, expand your client base, and generally represent your company in a positive manner. Some basic tips for working a room are:

- Don't be the first one to arrive unless you are hosting the party.
- Survey the room before you enter.
- If you have a drink, hold it in your left hand so your right hand is free.
- Avoid eating. It is difficult to talk, eat, and shake hands. Eat before you go! The worst thing you can do is to load up your plate and act like this is your last meal.
- Don't cluster in the corner with the only person you know! Move around the room, offering to shake hands and introducing yourself. Take the initiative. Most people will be glad you did.
- Focus on the other person. Smile and be friendly.
- Sell yourself with a sound bite—something interesting about yourself. For example: "I'm John Martin, the new admissions coordinator at Marion Hospital."
- Don't look around the room while you're talking to a person. Look at the person as though he or she is the most interesting person in the room. Use the person's name.
- Don't talk about politics, make fun of a state, or tell religious or ethnic jokes. You never know whom you might offend.
- Don't talk about your health.
- Converse a few minutes, excuse yourself and move on.

Dining Etiquette

In this brief space we cannot discuss everything you need to know about etiquette. We hope you know the basics such as: chew with your mouth closed, keep your elbows off the table, pass food to the right, cut your meat only one piece at a time, butter only one small piece of bread at a time. The finer points of etiquette have to be studied, however, if you are going to move up the ladder.

Read a good etiquette book and take it seriously. Research shows that only about 12 percent of new hires are skilled in the social graces. This may mean the difference in great success or failure. Excellent manners will set you apart early in your career.

As part of your interview, you may be taken to a nice restaurant. Order something that is easy to eat and not the most expensive thing on the menu. Figure 4.1 is a diagram of a formal table setting. Study it carefully so you will know what to do if you are dining at a formal restaurant. Starting at the outer edge, use the appropriate fork with each course. A good rule to remember is: Solids on the left, liquids on the right.

Formal place setting.

Top row, left to right;

Butter spreader, Bread-and-butter plate, Salt and pepper shakers, Menu card, Dessert spoon and fork, Water goblet, Champagne flute, White wine glass, Red wine glass, Sherry glass

Bottom row, left to right;

Fish fork, Dinner fork, Salad fork, Place card and napkin, Place plate, Salad knife, Dinner knife, Fish knife, Soup spoon, Cocktail fork

If you leave the table, place your napkin on your chair. When you finish your meal and are leaving the table, fold your napkin loosely and place it back on the table.

When women approach or leave the table, men should stand. If it is a business occasion, women should stand at the beginning of the meal and shake hands as the men are doing. Women do not need to stand when someone leaves the table or returns. Men should help the woman to their right with her chair and then help the woman on their left if no one else is doing so.

There is much to learn enroute to developing a professional presence. You probably will make some mistakes. Learn from them and keep working until you are comfortable in any setting.

References

Morem, Susan. (1997). *How to Gain the Professional Edge: Achieve the Personal and Professional Image You Want.* New York: Better Books.

Sabath, Ann M. (1998). *Business Etiquette: 101 Ways to Conduct Business With Charm and Savvy.* Santa Barbara, CA: Career Press.

Seitz, Victoria. (2000). *Your Executive Image: The Art of Self-Packaging for Men and Women.* Madison, WI: Adams Media.

Thompson, Jacqueline. (1994). *Image Impact.* New York: Bristol Park Books.

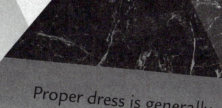

CAPSTONES

FOR PROFESSIONAL PRESENCE

Proper dress is generally tailored.

▲

Body language sends out signals, and you must pay close attention to it.

▲

Professional presence and image encompass posture, hygiene, clothing, stance, and grooming.

▲

Trendy clothes, suits, and jewelry are to be avoided. Besides, they can be pricey and may not be stylish for long.

▲

At business meetings and parties, circulate and get to know as many people as possible.

▲

A sense of professionalism is projected in your walk, stance, and dress.

▲

Proper dining etiquette is essential to a professional image.

▲

Business-casual does not mean shorts and tee-shirts.

CHAPTER 5

Professional Communication

I see communication as a huge umbrella that covers and affects all that goes on between human beings. Once a human being has arrived on this earth, communication is the largest single factor determining what kinds of relationships he makes with others and what happens to him in the world about him. How he manages his survival, how he develops intimacy, how productive he is, how he makes sense, how he connects with his own divinity—all are largely dependent on his communication skills.

VIRGINIA SATIR

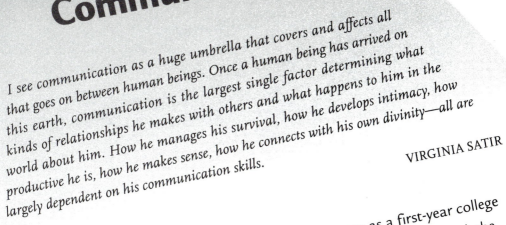

One of the earliest pieces of advice given to me as a first-year college student was this: "If you can effectively read, write, and speak the English language, there is nothing you can't accomplish; for understanding this language, you can learn all that you will ever need to know to get on in this world." I held those words close to me and grew to know that this advice was truly one of the most precious pearls of wisdom ever spoken. The ability to communicate on all levels is one of the—if not THE—most essential tool needed for success in today's workforce.

51

Every day we engage in some type of communication. If you are alive, you can't help but communicate. Even when you are not speaking, if you are in the presence of another person, you are communicating some type of message. As a matter of fact, we spend more than 61 percent of our waking time engaged in some form of communication (Adler et al., 1989). Communication is so important in the world of work today that oral communication skills, listening skills, and written communication skills are three of the top five factors that help graduating college students obtain employment (Curtis et al., 1998).

In Brownell's article (1991) on middle managers, she discusses communication in the following manner:

"No other managerial competence is so directly tied to job success. Every one of your daily activities—motivating, influencing, explaining, delegating, coaching—depends upon communication effectiveness."

In an effort to understand more about verbal, nonverbal, and written communication, this chapter will explore the following topics:

▲ A working definition of communication

▲ Why we communicate

▲ The power of communication and language

▲ The communication process

▲ Roles in communication

▲ Barriers to communication

▲ Types of communication

Communication Defined

Communication is not something we *do to* people. It is something done *between* people. Communication can take a variety of forms, such as oral speech, the written word, body movements, and even yawns. All of these actions communicate something to another person. In defining communication, we can say that it is continuous, irreversible, and unrepeatable.

COMMUNICATION IS CONTINUOUS

If you are in the presence of another human being, you are communicating. It can't be helped. If you walk into the back of a crowded room, sit by yourself, and never open your mouth, you still are communicating. The message might be unclear, but you are communicating. The message to some may be that you want to be alone. To others, it may be that you are shy. To still others, the message may be that you do not mix well with people. In reality, you may sit at the back of the room because you have to leave early and do not want to disturb others. The simple fact remains: You are communicating.

COMMUNICATION IS IRREVERSIBLE

Once you have said something, it cannot be taken back. You can apologize for it, explain it, and try to make it go away, but the fact that it was said can never be erased. The most important lesson here is that we should know what we are saying before we say it. Relationships have been lost, feelings hurt beyond repair, and friendships derailed because of words uttered before thinking. This lesson is of ultimate importance as you begin your new career.

COMMUNICATION IS UNREPEATABLE

"Unrepeatable" is the most abstract of the terms that describe communication, but it is of immense importance. You have only *one* time to make the impact you want to make. Once you have said the words, they will never mean the same thing again. Think of the first time a person said to you, "I love you." You may have heard it 100 times since, or you may not have heard it again. The fact of the matter is this: It may mean more now or less now, but it will never mean to you what it meant to you the first time you heard it. You will not feel the same emotion again that you felt the first time you heard those words from that person. This is important to remember because you will have many opportunities to present information, reports, and ideas to people, and your first impression may be the one that carries your project and career forward.

ΛDVIＤＥ FＲOM Λ MＥNTOＲ

Steve Brannon, Consultant

C.C.S. Fundraising, New York

Writing and speaking are two of the most important skills that any human can possess at any time, in any profession, anywhere on earth. Seize the opportunity to learn everything through continuing education, seminars, conferences, and meetings that promote, teach, and encourage effective writing and speaking skills.

In today's ever-changing world, you must be open to every possibility. Learn computers and electronic communication devices. Keep up with the latest developments and trends, but master the gentle art of conversation. Email has replaced the epistolary arts; therefore, study writing! It is not enough to know how to communicate electronically. One must know what to say and how to

say it effectively. Ideas, and the effective expression of them, can carry you up the corporate ladder overnight, literally!

In the world of work, you will learn that interpersonal skills are simply mandatory. It's all about people. Electronic devices allow us to get the basics out of the way quickly, freeing up more personal time to be "present" with each other. Never allow email and faxes and computers to replace the human art of communication.

Why We Communicate

Communication gives us our identity. We learn who and what we are by our association with the people around us. Through our communication we learn our language and many of our values, and, for the earlier part of our lives, it is how we learn our self-perception.

The study of communication has been around for hundreds and hundreds of years. As early as the 1200s, Frederick II, Emperor of Germany, was conducting experiments on infants to study their communication habits.

He bade foster mothers and nurses to suckle the children, to bathe and wash them, but in no way to prattle with (speak to or touch) them, for he wanted to learn whether they would speak the Hebrew language, which was the oldest, or Greek, or Latin, or Arabic, or perhaps the language of their parents of whom they had been born. But he labored in vain because all of the children died. For they could not live without the petting and joyful faces and loving words of their foster mothers. (Ross & McLaughlin, 1949, in Adler et al., 1989)

The U. S. Government conducted tests like this on infants until the middle of the 20th century. The results were much the same. The babies who were not touched, cradled, or nurtured literally withered and died.

These studies and others give us reason to value communication and reason to strive to become more effective communicators. We communicate for many reasons including

identity
survival
establishing relationships
gaining knowledge
enjoyment
entertainment
expressing opinions
obtaining our wishes
altering emotions
promoting health and reduce stress

The more we learn about communicating verbally, nonverbally, and in writing, the stronger we will become in each of these areas and the more fulfilled our lives will become.

The Power of Communication and Language

The power of words is staggering. Words can make a person's day or break a person's spirit. Words change nations, free masses, and even start wars. The most interesting thing about words is that they must have a medium. They must be written or spoken. Here is where you come into the picture. In truth, the statement, "the power of words," is an misnomer. Words have little power until they are used by humans. We determine how words and phrases are to be used and, in turn, we determine their power.

For example, if we were to begin a conversation with an employee or a co-worker by saying, "The job you did on the AT&T account last week was some of the worst work I have ever seen," we are setting up the entire conversation for failure. Because communication is *irreversible* and *unrepeatable*, we have inflicted damage from which neither party will soon recover. If, however, we had begun the conversation on a more positive note, using language that was constructive instead of destructive, the outcome could have been entirely different. The power of words is indeed staggering.

Roles In Communication

The two major roles in the communication process are the *communicator* and the *listener*. Poor communication is one of the most common complaints in the world today. It seems that every business magazine you pick up contains some information about improving communication skills.

The hardest part about opening and improving the lines of communication is that it takes everyone in the environment working together to have a noted impact. But just because more people are talking, this does not mean that better communication is happening.

According to Krackhardt and Hanson (1993), "When it comes to communication, more is not always better." After studying the banking industry, they found that *"more* communication ties did not distinguish the most profitable branches; the *quality* of communication determined their success." Branches with two-way communication between people of all levels were found to be 70 percent more profitable than branches with one-way communication.

Success in Communication

Following are some tips and strategies for the various forms of communication.

PUBLIC SPEAKING

To improve the quality of your verbal communication skills in formal situations such as *public speaking and speaking with groups* of people, use these simple strategies:

- Be sincere.
- Be clear, accurate, and detailed.
- Mean what you say, and say what you mean.
- Choose your words carefully.
- Use examples and stories to clarify your point.
- Ask for feedback during the discussion.
- Get to the point.
- Emphasize your main points.
- Pay attention to others' feelings and emotions.
- Respect others and their opinions.
- Don't use language that is threatening or demeaning to you or others.
- Work to put other people at ease.
- Remember the power of silence; force yourself to listen.
- Pay attention to your nonverbal communication.

VERBAL INTERPERSONAL COMMUNICATION

To enhance your *verbal interpersonal communication* skills:

- Look directly at the person with whom you are communicating.
- Speak simply, clearly, and precisely.
- Be concrete, concise, and correct.
- Be culturally sensitive, tolerant, and patient.
- Use colorful, vivid terms to create visual images.
- Don't be afraid to communicate your feelings.
- Don't dominate the conversation. Communication is a two-way event.
- Listen.
- Ask questions.
- Work to establish positive rapport with the other.
- Be honest and objective to foster trust.
- Use tact and diplomacy.

NONVERBAL INTERPERSONAL COMMUNICATION

To enhance your *nonverbal interpersonal communication* skills:

- Use appropriate facial expressions.
- Make eye contact with the person with whom you are communicating.
- Respect the other person's personal space or "bubble."
- Use a *confident* handshake (harder is not always better).
- Be careful with touch if you are a "touchy-feely" person. Others may misinterpret your touch.
- Recognize that clothing and hygiene are strong nonverbal indicators, and pay attention to grooming.
- Pay close attention to your gestures and body movement, such as posture, needless movement, and nervous energy.

▲ ▲ ▲

LISTENING

To enhance your *listening* skills:

- Stop talking.
- Don't give up too soon. Give the communicator a chance.
- Give the communicator your undivided attention; concentrate on what is being said.
- Leave your emotions outside of the communication process; control your anger and even your happiness, as both can cloud issues.
- Listen to *how* something is being said.
- Listen to what is *not* being said; listen between the lines.
- Avoid jumping to conclusions; withhold judgment until the message is complete.
- Ask questions along the way.
- Judge the message, not the messenger.
- Listen for the main ideas.
- Don't interrupt. Let people complete what they are saying.
- Give the communicator appropriate nonverbal signals, such as eye contact and nods, to indicate that you are listening.

Learning verbal, nonverbal, and listening skills in formal and interpersonal settings can help you advance rapidly in your career. All three are skills that few people do well. If you are among those who use them skillfully, you will be richly rewarded in your new career.

▲ ▲ ▲
WRITTEN COMMUNICATION

Almost every work setting requires varied types of communication. Seldom will you work in a situation in which you are required to engage in only verbal communication. To communicate successfully in writing, the three general steps in the process are: the draft, the review and revision, and the proof.

Drafting the Document

> Quite simply, and to many novice writers' chagrin, there's no magic formula for writing a draft. There is no right way to go about it, but on a positive note, there is also no wrong way to go about it. The only goal at this stage is to get something on paper or on your computer screen. (Allen, 1998)

As you begin to write your memo, letter, or report, you may face what many call writer's block. This is common for some people. The key to moving past the block and getting on with your work is to just start writing. It does not have to be perfect or in final form. Just write. Here is a strategy that is useful to some people.

1. Begin by considering whether your document is supposed to inform, persuade, entertain, or have some other purpose.
2. Think about your intended audience.
3. Consider what research sources, if any, you will use.
4. Jot down your major thoughts in an outline form.
5. After you have your major points, go back to point 1 and begin to explain that point. Then move to point 2, and so on.

There is no right or wrong way to draft a document, bu the more planning you do, the easier it will become.

Reviewing and Revising the Document

Once you have completed your draft, read it several times to see if it flows. Does it make sense to you? Have you spelled out your major points? Have you explained those points in detail? Have you supported your ideas with research (if needed)? People who write often and deal with the same document many times can easily become immune to it. This is a good time to get a trusted colleague or friend to look at the document and made constructive comments.

While revising and reviewing your document, pay close attention to your grammar, syntax, punctuation, spelling, and style. Producing a memo or a proposal with obvious errors is inexcusable.

Proofing the Document

Now that you have completed your draft, enlisted assistance, and made your final corrections, spend a few moments reading the document again. Reading it aloud or having that trusted colleague or friend read it again may be helpful. Only one spelling error, one incorrect date or fact, or one misspelled name can damage your credibility.

FORMS OF WRITTEN COMMUNICATION

Examples of written communication in the workplace are the memorandum, the business letter, email, and reports.

The Memorandum

One of the most common types of workplace documents is the office memorandum, or memo. Memos are written for people *inside* the office, whereas business letters are usually written for people *outside* the office setting. Memos usually are shorter than letters and get straight to the point. Most memos use the format given in Figure 5.1.

The Business Letter

A business letter is usually sent to someone outside of the office. It is more formal than a memo or an email. Typically, business letters are written in full block format, meaning that all of the margins are justified on the left and will have the elements shown in Figure 5.2.

Electronic Messages (Email)

Email has almost taken over every type of business communication from memos to letters to formal reports. This can be advantageous for you and the receiver because it saves time and paper and can have a much quicker turnaround. Emails also can be tracked and you can have an electronic return receipt to establish when the receiver opened the email. A drawback of email is that once you click "Send," the document is gone. This means that you have to make sure your document is correct before you send it.

There is no set format for an email. You could use the memo format, or another standard business format. In any case, when sending emails:

- Do not send an email that you would not want everyone to see. Most email is *not* confidential.

Standard format for memos.

MEMORANDUM

To: Jane Doe,   *(the person who receives the memo)*
           Vice President of Sales

From: John Harris, *JH*   *(the person sending the memo; note the*
           Director of Marketing   *handwritten initials here)*

Date: June 10, 2001   *(date of the memo)*

Subject:* Annual Sales Meeting   *(what the memo is about)*

C: Jonathan Blackwelder   *(the person(s) to whom the memo is being sent*
                                        as secondary receivers. Not all memos are copied.)

Body of the memo   *(with no greeting such as Dear Ms. Doe, or Jane)*

                      (No signature is needed at the end of the memo; the signature or initial
                      is placed after your name in the heading, as in the example above.)

Enclosure   *(This term appears at the bottom of the memo if you are enclosing*
                      something with the memo.)

Attachment   *(This term appears at the bottom of the memo if you are attaching*
                      something to the memo.)

* On some memos, instead of the word "subject," you will see "RE:" which means "Regarding."

- Don't use email at work for private or personal messages.
- Don't let your emotions get the best of you. When email was not available, we had more time to think about our words and meanings. Email has given us the ability to spout off hastily and to SHOUT, using capital and bold letters. Be careful.
- Finally, if your company owns the computer on which you work, the company has a right to see what is on the hard drive.

ACE EDUCATIONAL SUPPLIES

1234 Elm Street, Upper Saddle River, NJ 12345, 123-456-1234

(If the business does not have a letterhead you will have to type the name and address. Some businesses also include fax and email numbers.)

June 12, 2000   *(the date the letter is written)*

Dr. Larry Smith   *(the address to whom the letter is being sent)*
New Jersey School District
1234 Elm Street
Lakewood, NJ 12354

Dear Dr. Smith: *(The salutation opens the letter with "Dear Mr., Mrs., Ms., or Dr.,"*
                          followed by a colon.)

Xxxxxxxxxxxxxxxxxxxxxxxxxxxxxxxxxxxxxxxxxxxxxxxxxxxxxxxxxxxxxxxxx. Xxxxxxxxxxxxx
xxxxxxxxxxxxxxxxxxxxxxxxxxxxxxxxxxxxxxxxxxxxxxxxxxxxxx. Xxxxxxxxxxxxxxxxxxxxxxxxxxxxxxxxx
xxxxxxxxxxxxxxxxxxxxxxxxxxxxxxxxxxxxxxxxx.

Xxxxxxxxxxxxxxxxxxxxxxxxxxxxxxxxxxxxxxxxxxxxxxxxxxxxxxxxxxxxxx. Xxxxxxxxxxxxxxxxxxxx
xxxxxxxxxxxxxxxxxxxxxxxxxxxxxxxxx.

(Body of letter, using accurate, error-free information)

Sincerely,   *(The closing. You also could use "Sincerely yours," "Yours truly,"*
                     "Respectfully," or another acceptable closing. The closing is followed
Roberta A. James   *by a comma.)*

Roberta A. James   *(Your name. You should leave four spaces for your signature between*
                          the closing and your typed name.)

BW/rj   *(The initials indicate who composed the letter (BW), followed by*
               who typed it (rj). These are separated by a slash.)

c: Arnold James   *(If the letter is going to be sent (copied) to anyone else, names of those*
Patricia Sampson   *copied follow the c: heading.)*

Enclosure(s)   *(If you plan to enclose information with the letter, "Enclosure,"*
                       "Enclosures," "Enc.," or "Encl." will end the letter.)

Reports

Whether you are an educator, a fire-fighter, a doctor, a lawyer, a landscaper, or an independent business person doesn't matter. You probably will be required to write some type of report over the course of your career.

> Most reports simply document routine business operations. Occasionally, however, a report galvanizes society into action with its findings or recommendations. The report on the Challenger disaster resulted in a complete overhaul of the shuttle system. (Boiarsky & Soven, 1995)

Reports are written to keep people who are involved in projects informed about progress, completion, costs, effects, and/or complications. A report, like a business letter, a memo, or email, has the purpose of informing or persuading. When writing reports, you should know the intended audience, the purpose of the report, what research or ancillary documents will be required as support materials, what graphics, if any, will be needed, and, of course, you must know the details about which you are writing.

Reports vary in style and format. The following are general considerations.

Introduction

Purpose of the report

What the report will cover?

Definition of terms with which readers are unfamiliar

Overview of the situation, problem, or challenge

Who is involved with the project and why?

What has been done to date?

What is being done currently?

What are the future plans?

What are the costs?

What are the benefits?

What are the pitfalls?

What are the recommendations to date? Why?

Results

Summation

Questions/Comments

If you are asked to write a report and are unfamiliar with the process, ask to see a copy of a previously completed report that you can use as a model. Again, ask trusted colleagues and assistants for help in reviewing, revising, and proofing the report.

References

Adler, R., Rosenfeld, L., and Towne, N. (1989). *Interplay: The Process of Interpersonal Communication* (4th ed.). New York: Holt, Rinehart and Winston.

Allen, J. (1998). *Writing in the Workplace*. Boston: Allyn and Bacon.

Boiarsky, C., and Soven, M. (1995). *Writings from the Workplace: Documents, Models, Cases*. Boston: Allyn and Bacon.

Brownell, J. (1991). Middle Managers Facing the Communication Challenge. *Cornell Quarterly,* February 1.

Curtis, D., Winsor, J., and Stephens, R. (1998). National Preferences in Business and Communication Education. *Communication Education,* Vol. 38, January, p. 11.

Krackhardt, D., and Hanson, J. (1993). Informal Networks: The Company Behind the Chart. *Harvard Business Review,* July–August, pp. 105–111.

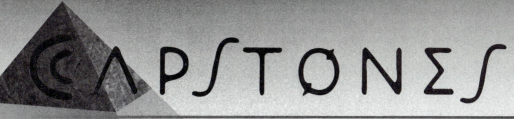

CAPSTONES

FOR EFFECTIVE COMMUNICATION

The use of words is powerful.

▲

Proofing written documents is essential.

▲

Nonverbal communication speaks loudly.

▲

Email is not private, so senders must use it judiciously.

▲

Effective verbal, nonverbal, and written communication is essential in any workplace.

▲

Communication is continuous, irreversible, and unrepeatable.

▲

Communication is a two-way event involving the sender and receiver of the message.

▲

Effective communication skills can help you move up in your career.

▲

Listening is as important as speaking in many communication situations.

The Interview Process

Opportunities are usually disguised as hard work, so most people don't recognize them.

ANN LANDERS

F inding the right job is hard work! You may have several interviews before you find the job you want, and you probably will spend many hours preparing for these interviews. In the beginning, you should go to all interviews even if you know in advance that you don't want the job. The more you interview, the more confident and comfortable you will become. Because the interview is the determining factor in getting a job, it must be taken seriously. Although an outstanding resume is important, it will not secure the job for you. The resume gets the interview; the interview gets the job!

To understand more about the interview process, preparing for the interview, social graces involved, and standard interview questions, this chapter will discuss the following topics:

▲ Preparing for the interview

▲ The first impression

▲ Questions you can anticipate

▲ Questions you might ask the interviewer

▲ The second interview

▲ Negotiating salary

▲ Follow-up techniques

▲ The offer—acceptance or rejection

Preparing for the Interview

Just as you prepare for exams, you will need to prepare for the interview. If you have done a careful job search, as we discussed in Chapter 2, you have information on the company that wants to interview you. If you don't, the first thing you need to do after you schedule an interview is to research the company. Interviewers usually are impressed if you know something about the company and are able to talk about it and ask intelligent questions. If you go to an interview knowing nothing about the company, you are not likely to get the job.

In Chapter 4, "Professional Presence," we discussed the importance of dress, grooming, posture, and body language. Now you can put these tips to work. You need to look your best because your appearance will affect your performance. If you look like a professional, you are much more likely to perform at your peak.

You need two interviewing suits. Both must be clean, pressed, and ready to wear. Rarely does a person get a job after only one interview. You may be called back the next day for another interview, and it is best if you have another interviewing outfit. Do not underestimate the importance of professional appearance. Your clothes should be prepared earlier so you can focus on the interview and not be worried about getting your clothes cleaned or shoes polished.

You should have several copies of your resume to take with you. Typically, only one person conducts interviews, but at times several people may interview you. Place your resumes and your job-search information on the company in a black or cordovan leather portfolio. Using your research on the company, make a list of questions you want to ask the interviewer. You should not engage in an interview without asking questions yourself. You are interviewing the company just as the company is interviewing you. Interviewers are much more impressed if they think you have researched the company and if you have questions to ask.

If you are not positive about the location of the company, you may want to make a dry run the day before. Showing up late to an interview is deadly!

Allow yourself at least half an hour more than you think you will need in case you get lost, traffic is heavy, or you can't find a parking place. On the other hand, don't arrive too early for an interview even if you have to sit in the car. Allow yourself time to go to the restroom before you get to the receptionist's desk. Check your appearance once more before heading to the interview.

Remind yourself of this cardinal rule of interviewing before you arrive: Interviewers are not interested in what the company can do for you; they are interested in what you can do for the company. Therefore, you must present your case on why you want to work for the company and the contributions you are prepared to make.

If you take someone with you to the interview, he or she should wait in the car. Under no circumstances should you take anyone inside with you.

The First Impression

You should greet the receptionist or administrative assistant warmly and with a smile. Some managers ask their assistants for their opinions about candidates. A good rule is to be nice to everyone. While you are waiting for the interviewer to call you, observe the atmosphere in the building and the attitude of the people. Does it look like a pleasant place to work? Do the people appear to be happy? Or do you hear people complaining and snapping at each other? Can you envision yourself working here? Remind yourself that you are interviewing this company too. You might go for several interviews before you are offered a job or before you find the job you want.

You can expect the interviewer to come to the reception area and get you, or the receptionist might escort you into the interviewer's office. As soon as the interviewer sees you, he or she begins to make a decision. Research shows that you have just 7 seconds to make the proper first impression. You literally send out verbal and nonverbal signals that determine how others see you. Although the interviewer may not realize this, you need to be aware of how important the first few seconds are to your success. In the first few seconds, the interviewer sees you, and using an eye sweep, takes in what you have on, your grooming, your posture, your smile.

- Are you confident?
- Do you appear to be comfortable in this environment?
- Are you glad to be there?
- Are you sincere?
- Are you impeccably groomed and dressed?
- Are you warm and friendly?

You should extend your hand and give the interviewer a firm handshake, looking him or her in the eye while offering a warm and pleasant greeting. Now the interviewer has more information. Is your voice strong and pleasant? Is your handshake firm and confident? The interviewer is taking in your facial expressions, gestures, energy, and enthusiasm. Instinctively, the interviewer is sizing you up just as you are forming your own opinions about what kind of person this is. Before you go to the interview, practice the first 7 seconds in front of a mirror so you can see yourself coming across as confident, friendly, positive, and energetic.

You should be especially aware of the messages your eyes send. Eyes should be focused, engaged, and interested. Use your eyes to convey your sincerity and interest in the other person and the job. Your resume sent a message that caused this company to want to interview you. Now *you* are the message! You must be in control of the total package that greets the interviewer and makes that all-important first impression. Before going on an interview, you might want to reread Chapter 4, on Professional Presence.

The interviewer or the receptionist might ask if you would like coffee or something to drink. You should politely say "no." Your focus should be on what you are going to say and not on trying to balance a coffee cup. When you enter the interviewer's office, you could comment on a picture or a decorative object on his or her desk, but do not touch anything on the interviewer's desk or appear to read things on the interviewer's desk.

The interviewer probably will make small talk for a few minutes to give you time to relax and get comfortable. This is part of the interview, and you should avoid answering questions with a simple "yes" or "no." Elaborate on your answers without talking too much. For example, if the interviewer says, "I hope you had no trouble finding our building," you should not just answer "no." You might say, "No, I live near here, so I'm familiar with the location. Actually, I had a part-time job when I was a sophomore, and I brought materials to one of your managers from my department chair."

Interviewers often say, "Tell me about yourself." They are not looking for your life history as much as they are gathering background information on you and observing how well you can present information. As you converse with the interviewer, you should sit up straight and establish eye contact. You might say something like this:

> I grew up in Atlanta, Georgia, where I attended a large public high school. I played soccer, was Vice President of the Debate Club, and maintained a B+ average. As you know, I majored in Business Administration here at [your university or college]. I have been involved in extracurricular activities, but I have focused most of my extra time on my career. Each summer I have worked in my field and have held increasingly responsible jobs. I believe that I am ready to go to work and do an outstanding job.

The interviewer now can follow up on several topics, such as:

- What did you learn from debating?

- What did you learn from soccer that can be transferred to the workplace?
- Tell me about the summer jobs you held.
- You didn't mention your family. What kind of work are your parents involved in? Do you have brothers and sisters?

The interviewer then might ask you, "What do you know about XYZ Company?" This is a good opportunity for you to show how prepared you are. You could open your portfolio and tell the interviewer:

When I was researching XYZ, I found some interesting facts on your website. I know that you are an international company based in New York, and that you have over 4,000 employees. I learned that you have several divisions including food processing and distribution, restaurants, and contract food sales. In fact, this information is the reason I applied for a job with you through the University's Career Center.

My minor in college is Food Nutrition, and I think XYZ will be a great place to use that knowledge and the skills I developed during my internship with Global Foods. With Global, I worked in contract food sales, and I think I could be immediately effective in that area with XYZ.

You will, of course, have to adapt your answer to your own situation. There is no way to be completely prepared for questions an interviewer may ask. The key is to have anticipated the interviewer's questions and to be so comfortable with the message you want to convey about yourself that you sound confident and decisive. If you don't know an answer and can't even take a stab at it, just say, "I really don't know the answer to that question." This is okay once or twice, assuming the questions are not critical. As you talk, look at the interviewer and lean forward slightly, which indicates that you are listening intently.

Questions You Can Anticipate

After the first few minutes, the interviewer will begin asking additional questions. Some questions you might anticipate are:

- Why are you interested in [Microsoft, or Webber Hospital, etc.]?
- When did you decide on a career in _____?
- Tell me about your extracurricular activities.
- What are your strengths?

- What are your weaknesses?
- Do you have a geographic preference? Why?
- Are you willing to relocate?
- Do you have any job experience in _____?
- What can you do for the company?
- What other companies are you interviewing with?
- Tell me about a difficult problem you have had and how you solved it.
- Tell me about a time when you worked under stress.
- What kind of accomplishment gives you the greatest satisfaction?
- What are your long- and short-range goals?
- Where do you see yourself in five years?
- What one word best describes you?
- Describe one goal you have set over the past six months and how you went about accomplishing it.
- What is the biggest mistake you ever made? What did you learn from it?
- How do you deal with difficult people?

uestions You Might Ask the Interviewer

Although you should feel free to ask the interviewer an occasional question during the interview, the interviewer should lead during the first part of the interview. At the close of the interview, the interviewer may ask you if you have any questions. If you are not asked, you should say, "I have a few questions if you don't mind." Asking questions of the interviewer is impressive and indicates that you are interviewing the company as well. Some typical questions are:

- How would you describe a typical day in this position?
- What kind of training can I anticipate?
- To whom would I report?
- Will I have an opportunity to meet some of the people who would be my co-workers?
- Describe the training program.
- When will my first job performance evaluation take place?
- Why do you enjoy working for [Microsoft, or Webber Hospital, etc.]?

The Second Interview

If you make it to the second interview, you are considered a finalist in most cases. You can count on being in competition with at least four other people, so you can't totally relax at this point, but you can congratulate yourself on being marketable. If you got this interview after interviewing on campus, you can be sure the company is interested in you because the campus interviewer brings back only the top people.

During the second interview, you can expect to meet three or four more managers or supervisors, all of whom will ask questions. You may be required to take a battery of tests, to respond to "what if" scenarios, or to be interviewed by people with whom you would work. If you can locate someone who has been to a second interview with this company, this person can give you excellent information. The campus placement office might be able to identify someone for you—perhaps

ADVICE FROM A MENTOR

Bryan Delph, Geologist

Shell Offshore Incorporated,
New Orleans, LA

I believe that one of the most important aspects of the interview process is to be prepared for anything, but also to be yourself. The company has seen your resume and they are, apparently, pleased with your credentials. Now it is up to you to sell yourself, your talents, and your personality.

I believe that many people go into interviews and try to be "someone else." I think this is a huge mistake for two reasons. First, it may get you the job, but was it really *you* who got the job? What happens when you begin work and they find out that you are not what you appeared to be in the interview? Secondly, why would you want to work for a company where you have to pretend to be someone you are not?

My advice is to research the company, determine if the company has a philosophy that suits your personal values, determine if the daily work will be rewarding to you, take your best to the interview, and be yourself. If there is a "fit," you will get the job that suits you and the company.

a graduate who is working for this company. If so, call this person and ask for guidance and advice. Most will be glad to help you, as you are fellow alumni.

On the second interview you can expect to be taken to lunch or dinner, often by a younger member of the group. This may be a welcome relief from the grueling questions you might have encountered, but it is not a time to totally relax. Lunch and dinner are part of the formal interview. Formal interviews do not allow for "off the record" talk. At lunch, do not have a drink even if your host does. Simply order what you want without making a big deal of the fact that you are not having a drink. At dinner, have no more than one glass of wine if you typically drink alcoholic beverages.

If you are at lunch or dinner with several people, you should be a part of the conversation without talking too much or too little. Avoid controversial topics such as politics, religion, off-color jokes, or ethnic stories that might be offensive to someone. Organizations rely on personal relationships and communication.

Put yourself in the interviewers' place. Would you want to fly across country with someone who can't carry on a pleasant conversation? Would you like to have someone entertaining your clients who chews with his or her mouth open? Would you want someone representing you at a business cocktail function who is uncomfortable in social settings? Would you consider hiring someone who hasn't read a book since freshman literature and considers entertainment to be a six-pack in front of the Monster Vehicle Mud Race? The company is hiring someone who is going to be a colleague, and the interviewers are looking for a good match.

If you are having dinner or lunch with just one person, you might focus on learning more about him or her. Most people like to talk about themselves, so you can ask about their tenure with the company, where they went to school, what kinds of activities are available in the area, and where the best living accommodations are.

Order food that is easy to eat—not spaghetti or ribs—and pay careful attention to your manners. Order a mid-priced item, certainly not an expensive entrée. You can be assured that all of this is being observed. Interviewers are determining if you accomplished enough to represent them with clients and in public. If you are not comfortable with etiquette, study the rules carefully. Don't underestimate how important proper etiquette is to your advancing up the career ladder. Again, you might want to refer to Chapter 4 on Professional Presence prior to the interviewing process, because making the right impression is almost as important as your college record.

Negotiating Salary

If the company is interested in you, the interviewer might discuss salary and benefits with you on the second visit. Normally, you are advised not to bring up salary on the first interview. If, however, you detect that the company is not going to offer a salary that you can accept or if you have doubts that you are interested in working for that company, you might want to discuss this on the first interview.

If you have several options and you are not quite sure about this company, you might say: "I know it's not considered good interviewing technique to discuss salary on the first interview, but I'm interested in knowing what the range is for this position. I want to be fair to you and not accept another interview and have you go to that expense if we're too far apart."

At the end of the second interview, if the interviewer hasn't mentioned salary, you should bring it up. You want the company to make the first move on salary. If the interviewer asks you, "If we are to make you an offer, what kind of salary are you looking for?" you can counter with this statement: "What is the range for this position?" This will give you something to go on.

If the interviewer then says, "The range is $27,000 to $32,000," you know if you are interested and you also know you want to go on the high side of this range. If you have exceptional grades and experience and you feel confident that the company really wants to hire you, you can try for a salary higher than the range. Most companies can go higher if they really want a person.

Then you would respond, "Based on my educational background and my work history, I really expect to start in the $35,000 range"—and then negotiate from that point. You don't want to lose a really good opportunity haggling over $1,000. On the other hand, you have to live on this salary, and your early raises will be figured on your base, so it is important to negotiate a salary that you think is fair to you.

On the second interview, if salary has not been mentioned, you might say something like this:

> We haven't discussed salary and benefits and, of course, that's important to me. I'm very interested in this company and this job, and I know I can make a positive contribution. In fact, everything about this job and the people I will be working with appeals to me. Could you tell me about the financial considerations?

You should have a salary in mind that you must have and will not take less and be prepared to walk away and continue looking. Salary negotiation can be tricky. You have to know what you are worth and not overestimate what you are worth, and you have to be willing to speak up.

If you are uncomfortable talking about money, get over it! Practice with someone, and practice by yourself until you think you can comfortably discuss salary and benefits. You might ask a professor to help you determine a reasonable salary.

The second interview is also the time to get an in-depth description of benefits, if you can. If the salary is a little higher at one company but the benefits are poor, you might want to take the lower salary. Typical benefits that most companies offer are:

- *Health insurance.* (Sometimes benefits do not begin until an employee has been working for a certain period of time. Now is the time to ask.)

- *Life insurance.* (This is 1 1/2 times your salary as a rule with options to purchase more. If you are single, this is enough. Life insurance is not a good investment.)

- *Dental insurance.* (Most major companies offer dental insurance today.)

- *Paid vacation.* (Vacations in the beginning are typically 1 to 2 weeks, increasing with longevity.)

- *Sick days.* (Most companies allow a specified number of sick days. Be careful how you take them, because if you use all of them and you have not had a major illness, it looks bad on your record.)

- *Personal and other holidays.* (Some companies allow you a certain number of personal holidays to use as you wish as long as you have them approved. Most companies honor major holidays; the nature of some businesses, however, precludes this option. How important are Christmas Eve and Christmas Day with your family if you have only this time and you are in California and they are in South Carolina?)

- *Moving expenses.* (This is important if you have to move some distance and you have furniture. Some companies will not pay for your first move, so be sure to ask. Maybe this is a negotiable point, or maybe you don't want the job.)

- *Tuition reimbursement.* (Not all companies provide this benefit, but it could be important to you if you plan to seek a graduate degree.)

- *Profit Sharing or 401–K.* (These benefits are discussed in Chapter 13, on finances. If you can find a job that offers these benefits and it meets your requirements in other areas, these benefits are highly desirable.)

- *Retirement plan.* (More and more companies are offering profit-sharing and 401K plans in lieu of formal pension plans. If you take a job with a company with this plan, it is crucial to your future that you learn everything about the plan as soon as you can. If you can get printed information before you take the job, you should examine it carefully before making your final decision.)

- *Company car.* (New employees are given a company car only if they are going to travel for the company, usually as a salesperson. A company car is an excellent benefit if you are allowed to drive it for personal use. You don't have to make a car payment or insurance payments, pay for maintenance, or pay taxes—but you must travel and spend nights on the road.)

While you are asking questions, you might want to discuss the cost-of-living differential in, for example, San Francisco, where they want to send you, compared to where you live now. Of course, you have looked this up on the Internet, and you know that you must have more money to live in certain areas of the country. If you are not given a cost-of-living consideration, don't take the job.

Depending on the company, you may be offered other benefits. The ones listed above, however, are typical.

Follow-Up Techniques

Before you leave, establish a time by which you can expect to hear from the company. Normally this is no more than 1 or 2 weeks. If you are told to expect to get word in a week and you have not heard, consider calling the person who invited you to visit. You should not call several times, and never before the date you were told they would make a decision. If they are not interested in you, most companies send a form letter thanking you for your time and informing you that another person has qualifications more suited to the position. This is common practice, and you can expect this to happen to you a few times, so don't be overly concerned if you don't get the first job for which you interview.

After the interview, immediately send a handwritten note to the person who invited you to come. Thank the company for its interest in you, and, if you are interested in the position, indicate your interest in the job and your confidence in being able to make a positive contribution to the company.

The Offer—Acceptance or Rejection

An official offer normally is made in person or by telephone. If you know you want the job and you are happy with the offer, accept immediately. If you are considering other offers, ask for 2 or 3 days before giving an answer. In the interviewing process, you often will find that you don't have enough information at the time to make the best decision. You might have to accept anyway or lose a good opportunity.

Even if you accept a job orally, write a follow-up letter as a formal record of your decision. This letter should repeat the terms of employment, the location, the salary, expected reviews following the training period, and any other information the company has requested.

If you reject an offer, write a *handwritten* note to the company expressing your appreciation for the opportunity to have interviewed and stating that this was a difficult decision for you. You may want to interview with this company again someday, so do not burn your bridges.

References

Allen, Jeffrey G. (1988). *The Complete Q & A Job Interview* (2d ed.). New York: Wiley.

Kennedy, Joyce L. (1995). *Electronic Job Search Revolution* (2d ed.). New York: Wiley.

Marler, Patty, and Mattia, Jan B. (1995). *Job Interviews Made Easy.* Lincolnwood, IL: VGM Career Horizons.

Yate, Martin. (1995). *Knock 'Em Dead: The Ultimate Job Seeker's Handbook.* Holbrook, MA: Adams Publishing.

CAPSTONES

FOR INTERVIEWING

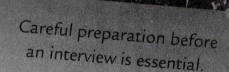

Careful preparation before an interview is essential.

▲

Part of this preparation includes researching the company.

▲

Your best communication skills are necessary.

▲

Excellent grooming and professional presence and etiquette are paramount.

▲

Careful preparation will contribute to an excellent first impression.

▲

The salary has to be satisfactory to you. Sometimes this can be negotiated.

▲

The follow-up consists of appropriate letters and documentation.

UNIT TWO
Professional Development

ADVICE FROM A PEER

Chris Latusky,

Graduate, Associate of Arts, General Studies
Community College of Southern Nevada, Las Vegas

For more than 20 years, I worked in banking. I supervised and provided leadership to hundreds of people during my career. One day, however, because of a merger, I no longer had a job. There I was, married, "older," and no college degree. There was only one choice for me.

I returned to college for many reasons: to get advanced training, to learn more about technology, to meet new contacts, and to grow as a person. As a recent graduate from the Community College of Southern Nevada, I would offer this advice to you: Learn how to deal with change and go with the flow.

After changing careers, I have learned that the only certainty in the world of work is change. Although I have specific duties with my job today, I never know what each day will hold. One day I might be working with a group of students to outline a tutoring session for math. The same afternoon, I could be ordering books for a new computerized tutorial lesson. Tomorrow, I might spend the entire day on accounting matters or could easily be running the front desk. Change happens every day.

Shortly after I began my new job, the director who hired me returned to teaching. A new director was hired, I was promoted, we changed computer systems, hired a new full-time assistant, and moved to another location—all in the course of 6 months. I could have had a nervous breakdown, but I learned to accept change and its challenges and joys as a daily part of life in the world of work.

Diversity in the Workplace

I am a citizen, not of Athens or Greece, but of the world.　　SOCRATES

Since the beginning of time, people have been forced to deal with individuals who are different from themselves, individuals of the other gender, from different tribes and different geographic locations with different traditions and lifestyles. These dealings have not always been peaceful. Most, if not all, altercations, disagreements, and wars can be traced to an issue of how to deal with people who are different from one another. Some choose to learn from one another and either coexist or grow together as a common group, whereas others choose to fight with one another, with the victor either annihilating or enslaving their captives.

The business world today is not much different. Internally, companies must deal with hundreds of different cultures in a positive manner or face failure. Externally, companies are compelled to carve out their niche in the market-place and either work toward coexisting with other companies in their segment of the market or competing for the purpose of annihilation or takeover.

In this chapter we discuss how culture impacts the workplace. Specifically, we will look at:

▲ The idea of a culture of one

▲ Who you are

▲ Who your colleagues are

▲ Adjusting to cultural diversity

Σ ach individual brings to the workplace a unique culture determined by a distinctive set of values, beliefs, and customs. Everything we have experienced prior to entering the workplace influences our work ethic. Our race, our nationality, where we live, where we went to school, the level of our education, our religion or lack of religion, our friends, our relatives, and our experiences and opportunities—all play a role in who we are and, to some extent, dictate what we will bring to our career.

Culture is learned. People are born into a culture, but their culture is not a physical trait, such as eye color or hair texture. You probably developed, or absorbed, most of your personal culture from your family. The process is almost like osmosis in plants; it is as though culture seeps gradually through your skin. Many of the beliefs and values you embrace have been passed from one generation to another. (Montgomery et al., 1999)

We view our world and respond to that world through the filters of our culture. Recognizing these filters is important to understanding why you think and act the way you do. For example, a White 50-year-old woman with a fifth-grade education from New York City would be looking at a situation through the filters of gender, age, education, and regionality. Understanding these filters enables her to determine the validity of her perceptions and adjust her responses correctly.

To continue this example, if this woman had recently left employment with a company because the corporate culture had shifted and it no longer welcomed people without at least a high-school diploma and, in addition, the company was looking for a way to remove her because, as a result of her length of service, she was being paid a higher wage than the current market rate, she would be bringing baggage from this company regarding her treatment. Both she and her new employer would benefit from understanding how this experience has impacted her. Understanding her filters would enable both to do this.

Individual diversity in personal characteristics among those in your workplace comes from several sources: demographic differences, such as age, sex, culture, ethnicity, and language, and differences in personality and working and learning styles (Johnson & Johnson, 1994).

Demographic shifts in the workplace have a significant impact on the culture of an individual as well as the corporate culture. Differences in personalities, as well as individual working and learning styles, also influence individual and corporate culture and must be taken into consideration in every aspect of business.

Who Are You?

In *Managing Diversity*, Gardenswartz and Rowe (1993) equate the individual to an onion with layer upon layer of cultural teaching. They suggest that the following factors shape our identities.

1. Ethnicity—the ethnic group with which a person identifies and the person's native language.

2. Race—the racial group or groups with which a person identifies.

3. Religion—the organized denomination or sect to which a person subscribes or rejects.

4. Education—the level and type of learning a person receives.

5. Profession/field of work—the type of work a person is trained to do.

6. Organizations—groups or associations to which a person belongs or has belonged, such as the military, a scouting group, a labor union, or a fraternal organization.

7. Parents—the messages, verbal and nonverbal, a person's parents convey about ethnicity, religion, values, and cultural identity.

To fully understand who we are, in addition to these powerful cultural influences we must consider the various filters through which we view the world. All of these factors and filters shape our personalities as well as the strengths and weaknesses we bring to both our personal and professional worlds. They impact the kind of work we are meant to do, the kind of business, company, or corporation with which we should affiliate, and the work ethic we bring to that workplace.

ΛDVIÇΣ FRØM Λ MΣNTØR

James E. Farmer,

Group Director, Public Relations and Communications,
North American Vehicle Sales, Service and Marketing, General Motors Marketing

As a college student who will be entering the world of work soon, you need to know that many situations you will face will be vastly different from the college arena or place where your parents began their careers. Diversity is a frequently discussed issue and impacts every aspect of the workplace, from employment practices to promotion opportunities, from management styles to employee relations, from domestic relationships to global interaction. I can tell you without reservation that learning to celebrate diversity is an absolute must for success in your career.

As an African-American, I have experienced some "not too pleasant" people along the way, but I have learned to stay focused on my career goals and to be absolutely sure that I am being fair and consistent in my own workplace habits where diversity is concerned. I am responsible for my actions. I really can't do anything about other people's prejudices and biases, but I can be sure that I give every person a fair chance and that I judge them only on their character and their work performance. As a corporate executive for the world's largest corporation, I have had unlimited opportunities to interact with people from many diverse backgrounds. Therefore, on many occasions, I had to adjust in order to form

Who Are My Colleagues?

Your workplace, regardless of your discipline, is quite different from the workplace of your parents. People are working longer and, therefore, you will see a blend of generations that heretofore was seen only in some small family-run businesses that employed generation after generation of family members.

This blend of generations is leading to a major shift in business practices. What were once tried-and-true human resource practices are no longer working for everyone. Today's businesses must move away from cookie-cutter benefits packages and incentives to meet the needs of their multigenerational workforce. No longer can competitive businesses continue to expect lifelong loyalty from the "company man."

The workforce consists of Baby Boomers, Generation Xers, and the soon to enter Generation Yers. These three generations have distinctly different work ethics. Baby Boomers have been consumed with success, generally measured by income. Although not as company-loyal as their parents, they, too, have placed a lot of stock in the corporate world. They have lived their lives in pursuit of the American dream only to ask, as they approach their twilight years: "What has my life meant?" "What have I accomplished?"

ΛDVIϹƩ
CONTINUED.

solid relationships with people who are different from me. The difference might be religion or ethnic background; it might be race, international culture, or sexual orientation. My personal reward is getting past these differences and learning to appreciate people for who they are and for what they can contribute.

Prior to assuming my current position, I was Vice President for Corporate Communications at Saturn, "A Different Kind of Car Company." At Saturn, my primary responsibility was to protect and enhance the image of the company. That meant taking into consideration many factors that may impact our diverse customer base around the world.

I have taken my best practices from Saturn to my current position; a $100 billion enterprise, selling more than 5 million cars and trucks to a very diverse customer base. It is my responsibility to ensure that our advertising, promotions, and public relations efforts send the right message to a worldwide audience.

General Motors is an organization with manufacturing, sales, and dealers all over the world. I cannot afford to damage my personal career or the image of the company by carrying around prejudices and biases. I greatly encourage you to open up your minds and hearts to all types of people. You will be richly rewarded in your career and personal life.

Generation Xers are projected to go through seven or more career changes during their work life.

Representatives of Generation Y are more comfortable with themselves and their individual identity. This generation has a keen sense of technology. These people are racially diverse, optimistic, happy, free-spirited, sports-savvy, smart, and creative. They are less likely to follow the crowd. They seem to be less materialistic than the Xers and no longer equate success with money. They expect and demand a quality of life that Boomers and Xers were willing to put aside in their quest for success. The Y generation has grown up on the Internet and is more inquisitive and a lot more knowledgeable about media in general.

As the Baby Boomers move toward retirement, blending these three generations, coupled with globalization of the world, requires an understanding of cultural diversity unparalleled in human existence. Graduates entering the workplace have to be savvy about the differences in generations as well as the many cultures they will encounter in the workplace. They must become students of culture. To do this, they first must be comfortable with whom they are. This will enable them to accept and respect the diversity of their colleagues.

Adjusting to Cultural Diversity

Culture is the knowledge people share. Culture is an emergent process that is learned and becomes the inevitable channel for human behavior brought forth by this process. Culture establishes and maintains boundaries (Eitzen & Zinn, 1995), which are critically important in the business world. Ignorance of the boundaries of different cultures can lead to serious disagreements, and even war. Acknowledging that individuals have different cultures and then setting out to systematically learn about and understand others' cultures is the first step to harmony between you and those with whom you come into contact.

Culture has five components:

1. *Symbols*—items that stand for something, such as a country's flag
2. *Language*—a system of communication that provides meaning
3. *Values*—beliefs that typically are based on family traditions and religious beliefs
4. *Norms*—behavioral manifestations of values
5. *Sanctions*—ways by which a society enforces its norms

When a society adopts a set of norms that are upheld as valuable, it typically seeks a way to enforce these norms through formal laws (Montgomery et al., 1999).

To understand someone's culture, you must enter every relationship with an open mind, believing that all individuals have inherent worth and that we can learn something from everyone with whom we come in contact. If your mind is closed off to this approach to life, you will continuously face misunderstanding and confusion. The lessons to be learned will be all the more difficult, and you will miss out on a plethora of opportunities for you to grow.

> At one time or another, most of us have been exposed to the Golden Rule: "Do unto others as you would have them do unto you." As you work to improve and expand your knowledge of cultural diversity, it may help to look at this rule from a different angle. Consider the new version of the Golden Rule: "Do unto others as they would have you do unto them." (Montgomery, et al., 1999)

References

Eitzen, S., and Zinn, M. (1995). *In Conflict and Order: Understanding Society* (7th ed.). Needham Heights, MA: Allyn and Bacon.

Gardenswartz, L., and Rowe, A. (1993). *Managing Diversity: A Complete Desk Reference and Planning Guide.* New York: Irwin/Pfeiffer.

Johnson, D., and Johnson, F. (1994). *Joining Together: Group Theory and Group Skills* (5th ed.). Needham Heights, MA: Allyn and Bacon.

Montgomery, R., Sherfield, R., and Moody, P. (1999). *Cornerstone: Building on Your Best* (2d ed.). Upper Saddle River, NJ: Prentice Hall.

CAPSTONES

FOR UNDERSTANDING OTHERS

Each individual brings a unique culture to the workplace.

▲

Culture is the knowledge people share. The five components of culture are symbols, language, values, norms, and sanctions.

▲

Factors that shape our identities include ethnicity, race, religion, education, profession or field of work, organizations and groups or associations to which a person belongs, and parents.

▲

The workforce consists of Baby Boomers, Generation Xers, and the soon-to-enter Generation Yers. The work ethics of these three generations are distinctly different. To succeed, you must understand not only your own work ethic but also the work ethic of your colleagues.

▲

To understand someone's culture, you must enter every relationship with an open mind, believing that all individuals have inherent worth and that we can learn something from everyone with whom we come in contact.

▲

We all view the world through a set of filters consisting of gender, age, education, and regionality. These filters provide an important key to understanding why you think and act the way you do.

Workplace Politics and Civility

You don't turn integrity on and off. To have integrity, you must be like the guy who uses a butter knife when nobody is around.

WALLACE CARR

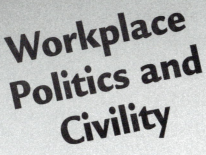

As you enter the workforce, you will become part of a group—unless you plan to open your own business in which you are the sole operator. The work group consists of people you work with. This group comes together for the sole purpose of fulfilling the goals and objectives of the company for which you work. Although you probably will not be instrumental in selecting those with whom you will work, you must nonetheless function in a productive manner with those in the company or you will fail at your job. As you may have experienced already in jobs you have held throughout your schooling, this is not as easy as it seems.

Learning to work successfully in the business world entails workplace politics and relies heavily on your ability to remain civil in dealings with co-workers, clients, and superiors. In this chapter we will look at some of the major areas that graduates will have to learn to navigate to be successful both personally and financially in the business world.

Specifically, this chapter will address:

▲ Developing a winning relationship with superiors and co-workers
▲ Dealing with office romances and other trouble spots
▲ Ethics in the business world
▲ Avoiding the rumor mill
▲ Moving up and being civil

argaret Wheatley, quantum physicist, author, and organizational theory consultant, notes in her book, *Leadership and the New Science* (1995):

> In the quantum world, relationships are not just interesting; to many physicists, they are all there is to reality. We do not exist in a vacuum. All things interact with each other. Successful human interaction is an essential part of your pathway to career success. With relationships, we give up predictability for potentials. Several years ago, I read that elementary particles were "bundles of potentiality." I have begun to think of all of us that way, for surely we are as undefinable, unanalyzable, and as bundled with potential as anything in the universe. None of us exists independent of our relationships with others. Different settings and people evoke some qualities from us and leave others dormant. In each of these relationships, we are different, new in some way.

To test the Wheatley theory, reflect on your own interactions with the individuals who are currently in your life. Are you the same person with each and every person with whom you interact? Think about the person you become whenever you go home to spend time with your family. Is that the same person your colleagues at school know, or the same person your boss and work colleagues know? In most cases we are different people based on our surroundings and the individuals with whom you come into contact. For this reason it is critical to choose to work for a company with which you share the business ideology. Otherwise you will be surrounded by co-workers with whom you have nothing in common and you will not respect your superiors.

Your ability to respect and work with others is the most important component of your work life. Benjamin Franklin stated that, "to be successful, you must do two things: surround yourself with outstanding people and read good books." If you respect those who surround you at work and have the same work ideology, you will be able to flourish in this facet of your life. If you are in an environment where this is not the case, you will be extremely uncomfortable and will find yourself either becoming someone you do not want to be or you will have to leave. Therefore, before you take a position, carefully examine the corporate culture and your superior and ask questions that will provide this information.

Most of our students are confused about the concept of the interview as a two-way street. You should carefully interview and critique your future company and immediate superior. Students are familiar with the concept of asking good questions so the interviewer will recognize that they are prepared for the interview, but we are suggesting that you take your part of the interview to a deeper level. Probe the interviewer about the company's corporate climate. Ask specifically about the company's ethics policy. Ask for an evaluation of the prevailing management styles of those with whom you will be working.

These questions, in our opinion, are equally important as questions about salary and benefits. If you do not have clear answers to these questions, we suggest that you delay your decision until you receive and completely understand the answers.

Developing a Winning Relationship with Superiors and Co-workers

If you select your job and your company properly, developing a winning relationship with your superiors should be relatively simple. In fact, it can be boiled down to one statement: Within the ethical confines of the company and yourself, do everything in your power to make your superiors and their superiors look good. Don't confuse this with "brown-nosing" or "sucking-up." That is not what we are suggesting. We are suggesting that you work hard to fulfill the goals and objectives set forth by your boss and by the company. If you do this, you will go a long way toward working well with your boss and co-workers. Some other helpful hints include the following:

- Spend time studying your superiors' work habits. Ask them what they expect of you. Remember that establishing a good relationship takes time.

- Keep your superiors informed. Nothing causes more problems than keeping superiors in the dark.

- Always follow up meetings with a written record of what you believe was said in the meeting. You can do this by providing your boss with minutes of your meetings.

- *Never* discuss your boss with co-workers. It *always* gets back to the boss.

- Keep your superiors' confidences. Do not pass along information unless you are specifically directed to do so.

- Once assignments are completed, always follow up to ensure that they meet their specifications.

Dealing with Office Romances and Other Trouble Spots

In your first post-college job, you may be placed in the unique situation of managing or supervising or leading people who are your age and older. Your ability to establish professional relationships with your staff and colleagues is important. Many of you will spend a lot of time at work trying to become proficient in your responsibilities and therefore will have little time left over to seek new relationships and friendships outside of work. The close proximity with your staff or co-workers often leads naturally to friendships. Although most people can relate stories of these relationships being successful, we encourage you to avoid them.

It is crucial that you establish what we call "professionally intimate" relationships. Professionally intimate relationships are those that enable you to learn about those with whom you work and to care about them as individuals, but without losing sight of the context in which your relationship must, first and foremost, be played out: in a professional environment.

You must strive to avoid situations that will lead to compromising circumstances. Encounters outside the workplace can lead to risky incidents. For example, because of the closeness in age between you and your co-workers and the long hours you will be working, it might seem normal to leave work and meet to have a drink or share a meal. Although in many cases this might be fine, the non–business-related environment might lead to a level of intimacy that will make it difficult for you to remain objective at work.

The old adage of not mixing business with pleasure is wise. This is not to say that colleagues cannot be friends, but you must not forget that these relationships have a different dimension, one that cannot be ignored or you will suffer the negative consequences at some time in your work life.

Office romances are easily established but not so easily concluded. If the romance is between you and a co-worker, the post-breakup atmosphere will be uncomfortable. If the romance is between you and a member of your staff or team, the results could end your career with the company and seriously damage your professional image.

As a result of laws regarding sexual harassment in the workplace, lines have been carefully drawn concerning workplace romances. It is *never* appropriate for you to establish a relationship with someone who reports to you. If you find yourself in a situation that seems to be heading in that direction, try to avoid it at all cost. If you believe this person is The One, your soulmate (and it seldom is), the least you should do is to change your work relationship by removing yourself from your current position, or the other person doing so, to eliminate the direct chain of command between you and your love interest. Although this will not protect you from the uncomfortable backlash when the relationship is over, it may protect you from legal action.

Many companies have a "no fraternization" clause in their corporate policies. This would lead to your dismissal as a consequence of such romances, even if legal action is not an issue.

Advice from a Mentor

Javier F. Ortiz,

Marketing Communications Specialist,
GTE Communications Corporation,
Irving, TX

Σ thics in the Business World

Theoretically, if everyone working for some company shares common goals, ensuring that the company is productive and successful, people should have absolutely no problem getting along. But

When planning for my career advancement, I make certain to use all of the resources I have. You have to pay attention to what is going on in the company, while at the same time completing the task at hand. So you have to learn how to do the daily job and plan for your future at the same time. You must stay informed about changes in the corporate structure and the political climate, gathering as much information as possible to ensure that you are properly prepared for opportunities that might present themselves. You must read and keep up on the issues in your industry. This will help you monitor the hiring climate in your field.

Always keep your resume updated and your career portfolio ready. I try to update mine every couple of months even when I'm not in the job market. This enables me to be prepared for my performance reviews as well as any opportunities for promotion that might present themselves suddenly.

College prepared me for my career by teaching me responsibility. I had to pass classes, do projects, study, and manage my priorities, some large stumbling blocks have to be overcome for this to happen. First and foremost, the company's goals and objectives must be in sync with your own goals and objectives. Before you accept a position with a company, you should study the company's philosophy. Does it treat employees the way you want to be treated? Does it treat customers the way you would like to treat your customers? Is the business ethic the same as your own?

Although we have preached this in all of our career courses and workshops, graduates continue to select positions based on salary rather than the company's ideology. Students who follow this path may soon find themselves disenfranchised from the company because the actions they must take on behalf of their company are in opposition to their own ethics and beliefs.

If this disparity becomes routine, one of two things will happen: The employee is forced to leave the company or has to compromise his or her own code of ethics, thereby becoming that which they hate, leading to a cycle of dissatisfaction and despair until the problem is corrected.

We've all observed individuals who chose to follow money instead of their conscience. They usually end up as burned-out cynics who care only about themselves and will step on anything or anybody who gets in their way. Generally speaking, regardless of what face they show to the world, they are extremely unhappy people.

In her book *Power Etiquette,* Dana May Casperson (1999) gives 13 hints for demonstrating your ethics in the workplace:

- Do not participate in gossip.
- Be courteous and respectful to superiors and to subordinates.
- Be positive and pleasant.
- Accept constructive criticism.
- Maintain personal dignity.
- Make an effort to preserve the dignity of another.

ΛDVIƆƐ CONTINUED.

all skills that help me greatly in my job today. I struggled with all of these skills at the beginning of my college career, but as the semesters went by, I got better at what I was doing. Every time I take a new position, I experience the same sort of learning curve, but now I realize that this, too, shall pass.

The most important advice I can give you about your career planning is always being honest with yourself. If you come to a place in your career where you don't feel comfortable, go with your gut feeling and either don't take the position/advancement or move on as quickly as possible. *Never* take a job if you don't have any interest in that job—that is a recipe for failure. And *always* accept responsibility for your actions.

- Keep confidences and maintain confidentiality.
- Show your concern for others.
- Give credit to those deserving.
- Be honest.
- Keep your word.
- Encourage and help others to do their best.
- Make practical and constructive suggestions for improvement.

Avoiding the Rumor Mill

Letitia Baldrige, in her *New Complete Guide to Executive Manners,* states, "Never go to bed at night wondering if you were a conversational gun in the slandering of a person's character or the endangerment of his/her future." Avoid, at all cost, becoming a part of the rumor mill. This may sound like an easy thing to do, but in reality it is human nature to want to be "in the know." To do this, however, you must engage in gossip, and a gossip is never trusted. One of the quickest ways to lose your credibility is to be seen keeping company with the corporate busybody.

Avoiding known gossipers is not in and of itself enough to avoid the rumor mill. There still will be ample opportunity to engage in gossip during your everyday interactions with co-workers. If you are present when a conversation based on speculation or rumor begins, we suggest that you either remove yourself quickly or state that, because the topic in question has not been substantiated, the conversation should not continue. It will not take too many such circumstances, in which you either leave or put a stop to the conversation, before your position about gossiping is well known and people will not include you.

The downside to this position is that people who refuse to be a party to gossip often find themselves the target of gossip. But this is a small price to pay for your personal integrity. You will have to make your own decision. Just be sure to weigh the consequences of your actions.

Moving Up and Being Civil

It's been said that if you find a job you really like, you will never have to work a day in your life. Advancing your career means falling in love with the job again and again. If you do not have a passion for what you do, no matter how hard you work, you will achieve only mediocrity in your life. Even though you may achieve financial success, those who have climbed the ladder of success for the wrong reasons invariably state that the victory lacks much.

To advance in your career, you must be prepared to remain in a constant state of learning and strive continuously to improve your skills. The most important lesson you can learn from your time in higher education is how to be a lifelong learner. Henry Ford stated, "Anyone who stops learning is old, whether at twenty or eighty. Anyone who keeps learning stays young." People who adhere to this philosophy also stay promotable.

Kahlil Gibran stated, "I have learned silence from the talkative, toleration from the intolerant, and kindness from the unkind." Some of the best lessons you learn can come from your biggest failures if you keep your eyes and your mind open. It is said that Theodore Roosevelt died with a book under his pillow, trying to learn until the last moment of his life.

Being excellent at what you do, however, does not guarantee that your career will advance as rapidly as you would like it to. Your ability to work with others within the political climate of your company is vital to your success.

> The continuous job search includes participation in the in-house politics
> and job-searching methods . . . . You must also understand the way your
> company policies dictate how promotions or lateral moves to other depart-
> ments are accomplished. (Breidenbach, 1998)

Seek advice from your mentor regarding the politics you should be involved in while climbing the ladder to success. If you abhor politics, as many of us do, understand that a certain level of political maneuvering is necessary to advance in your career. You can learn to be an artful politician by observing individuals in your company who are politically in tune with the corporate culture and who do not abuse the power they gain through their politicking.

To ensure that your career goals and expectations are reasonable, develop a plan to advance your career that includes the following:

- A list of skills necessary to attain a promotion
- A plan for developing your skills
- An overview of company policies governing the promotion
- Selection of a mentor to help lead you to the promotion
- A timeline for reaching the promotion.

A word of caution as you start your career is in order here: Be careful not to step on people as you climb your career ladder. Achieving your goal at the expense of a co-worker will lead to difficulties. Work toward the good of all those involved and do not take credit for something you did not do. If you are conscientious and a hard worker, your colleagues, in most instances, will be supportive and happy when you succeed. We all should learn from the Tibetan proverb that the good fortune of a friend is reason for great joy. Celebrate the advancement of your colleagues, and work hard to help them succeed while you are striving for your own success.

References

Baldrige, L. (1985). *Letitia Baldrige's New Complete Guide to Executive Manners.* New York: Macmillan.

Breidenbach, M. (1998). *Career Development: A 21st Century Job Search Handbook* (3d ed.). Upper Saddle River, NJ: Prentice Hall.

Casperson, D. (1999). *Power Etiquette: What You Don't Know Can Kill Your Career.* New York: AMA Publications.

Griffith, J. (1990). *Speaker's Library of Business Stories, Anecdotes, and Humor.* Upper Saddle River, NJ: Prentice Hall.

Izumo, G., Bishop, J., and Cole, K. (1999). *Keys to Workplace Skills.* Upper Saddle River, NJ: Prentice Hall.

Wheatley, M. (1995). *Leadership and the New Science.* Upper Saddle River, NJ: Prentice Hall.

CAPSTONES

FOR WORKPLACE CIVILITY

Ethical employees keep their word. ▲ Any plan to advance your career should avoid stepping on others. ▲ Advancing your career means falling in love with it over and over again. ▲ Your ability to respect and work with your colleagues is the most important component of your work life. ▲ Proper work relationships can be characterized as "professionally intimate." ▲ The company's goals and objectives must be in sync with your personal goals and objectives. ▲ Successful people surround themselves with outstanding people and read good books. ▲ Successful workers keep their superiors informed. ▲ The ethical employee does not participate in gossip. ▲ Ethical employees *never* discuss the boss with co-workers. ▲ The most important lesson you can learn from your time in higher education is how to be a lifelong learner.

CHAPTER 9

Networking and Mentors

Notice those chance events that occur at just the right moment, and bring forth just the right individuals, to suddenly send our lives in a new and important direction . . . there are no accidents.

JAMES REDFIELD, AUTHOR

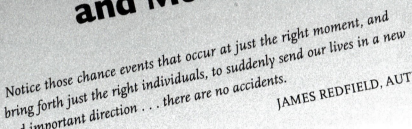

As you prepare for your entree into the professional world, you should surround yourself with outstanding individuals who will enable you to fulfill your potential and, consequently, your dreams. Developing a supportive network, spearheaded by a number of mentors, allows novices to build upon the education they received in college. A network will enable you to learn more than just knowledge. It will allow you to study and be tutored in the fine art of building your career.

You are entering the workforce at an opportune time. Individuals coming into the workforce during the 1980s and 1990s were referred to at times as the "me generation." They reaped the rewards or lack of rewards fostered by the perception that they lacked loyalty. Companies operating in an environment of lack of trust between employers and employees were hesitant to invest money in an employee who would leave for a higher salary. Companies also were pressured by a recession and had to cut back on their formal training programs. It was a "sink-or-swim" environment.

The growth of mentoring is a backlash against the cynicism that affects many corporate employees today (Elman, 1998). A properly conceived and administered mentor program can foster trust between employers and employees. It has long been known that mentoring benefits both individuals involved. The mentor receives satisfaction from seeing the growth of a protégé, gains incentive for career advancement, experiences more job satisfaction, and may gain a follower and a friend. The person being mentored receives encouragement, acquires new skills and knowledge, expands his or her professional network, receives advice on career planning, has a model to follow, and may gain a friend he or she admires and respects.

The development and expansion of a professional network is a crucial component of a mentoring relationship. Successful individuals understand the importance of developing a network that will give them an advantage over the competition. Unfortunately, some people abuse those they network with. Successful networking has to be a two-way street. If the relationship is to be successful, both parties must receive something from it. Younger, inexperienced people may wonder what they can bring to a mentoring or networking relationship. We advise our students to consider what *they* bring to the table. Could it be a willingness to do "grunt work" at an event sponsored by someone in the network, or perhaps keeping an eye on professional journals and literature and passing on articles of interest to someone in the network? You can contribute many things to your network.

If you are overwhelmed at the thought of choosing a mentor and developing a network, don't despair. This chapter is designed to enable you to:

▲ Define what a mentor is

▲ Identify qualities a mentor should have

▲ Understand how to work with a mentor

▲ Develop a working definition of networking

▲ Develop a strategy for cultivating your personal and professional network

▲ Understand how to make your network work for you

▲ Learn important networking skills

What Is a Mentor?

The history of traditional mentoring has been largely a one-on-one relationship between men. The term *mentor* arose in Homer's *Odyssey* from the name of King Ulysses's trusted friend, Mentor, who, in Ulysses's absence, nurtured, protected, and educated Ulysses's son, Telemachus. Mentor also introduced Telemachus to other leaders and guided his introduction into the world of politics and power. Therefore, a mentor's influence goes beyond that of just passing on knowledge to that of providing guidance in personal life skills that will help the individual develop in a holistic manner, thereby ensuring that the mentee is prepared to enter into the existing hierarchy.

The concept of having only one mentor in one's life has been replaced by the concept of having multiple mentors as society changed. Changes in the workplace over the last 100 years have greatly influenced the fine art of mentoring.

> To thrive in the modern workplace, employees have to create entire support groups of people inside and outside their companies, say executive recruiters and career counselors. (Rowland, 1999)

Mentors today come in all shapes and sizes and may provide guidance in only one specific area of an individual's life. Successful individuals recognize that "no man is an island," and, therefore, to reach their full potential, they must seek out people who are willing to mentor them in various areas of their professional and personal life.

Choosing mentors is only one step in building a network that will enable you to reach your full potential. You also must deliberately select and nurture relationships that will enhance your life. Building a personal network should not be left to chance. It should be viewed as an important component of your professional development.

As we prepared our list of industry professionals to invite to contribute to this book, we noted a couple of similarities in these highly successful individuals.

1. Their success was not an accident. They all systematically planned and prepared for success. All of the individuals quoted in this book developed both personal and professional goals. They did not wait for success to come knocking on their doors. They went out looking for it.

2. They all acknowledged that they had not reached their level of success alone. They recognized individuals in their life who provided guidance, encouragement, and knowledge that enabled them to reach their full potential.

A mentor for your work life is generally a well-respected individual who is farther along the career path, who provides informal training, shows you the informal systems, assigns you challenging work, and fosters your visibility in the organization (Hayes, 1996).

ΛDVIϚΣ FRØM Λ MΣNTØR

Maritza Correa,

Director of Convention Services
Disneyland, Anaheim, CA

Throughout my life, numerous individuals have impacted me greatly. I've always had professional and personal mentors—individuals who have encouraged me to be my best, and who have guided me in my professional development. They have also always impressed on me the importance of surrounding myself with excellent people.

One of the ways I have accomplished this is by taking part in professional associations. Professional associations are organizations designed to enable you to continue to improve your professional skills. Don't ever think that college is the end of your formal education. It is only the beginning. As a professional, your learning now comes in the form

of company training programs and development through professional associations. Professional associations enable you not only to stay on the cutting edge as far as knowledge goes, but they also enable you to build your network of professional acquaintances.

I've always been very active in a number of professional associations—first as just a member who participated in the educational

When looking for career mentors, do not limit yourself to only individuals within your organization. Look to individuals who are members of your professional associations and those who are in complementing organizations.

In *Career Transitions,* Cara DiMarco (1997) suggests that, in addition to a mentor who will guide you on your career path, you choose a *success mentor.* These are individuals whom you admire and consider to be successful in life. They may be in a completely unrelated field than you have chosen, but they have achieved significant success within their own arena. They may be famous people with whom you will not have a personal relationship but whom you can read about. Or they may be close relatives or someone at work. Lee Iacocca stated that one of the most important things he did as he shaped his career was to read biographies of great people and to integrate some of their practices into his own life.

Once you have identified someone who could serve as a success mentor, ask yourself, "What is it about the people or their lives that strikes me as successful?" How have they shaped their lives to become successful? Then develop strategies that enable you to emulate those characteristics in your own life.

If your success mentors are people you can meet and talk with, ask if they have a process or formula they follow in their life to which they attribute their success. If possible, integrate some of their process into your own life, keeping that which works and discarding the things that don't fit you personally.

Finding a mentor for your personal life, hobbies, volunteer work, and other interest areas is important too. As the percentage of people who experienced burnout during the 1980s and 1990s grew, it became increasingly evident to organizations that

ADVICE

CONTINUED.

programs and met others who were in my same position, but in companies from around the country and sometimes around the world. Eventually I moved into the leadership structure and now serve on the board and help to chart the future of the organization.

Professional associations have provided me numerous opportunities to increase my professional network. Now if I'm faced with a problem or if I need to hire someone, the network I've established through my professional associations is one of the first places I turn to for help. I've been very lucky to establish excellent business relationships with those I've met in my professional association. I've also been blessed with establishing some very close friendships with those whom I first met through associations. I've found that networking, like anything else, is only as good as what you make it. For me it has been crucial to my growth and success.

"all work and no play makes Jack and Jill one-dimensional." Single-dimensional people burn out at a much higher rate than do individuals who lead well-rounded lives. Learning how to balance home, work, and play is an important skill you need to learn, enabling you to live life to the fullest and to experience success in your career.

For mentors, look to people who share one or more interests in common with you and who appear to have balance in their lives—experiencing success in their professional lives and stability in their personal lives. Learn from them how they have managed to achieve balance in their lives.

▲ ▲ ▲

WHAT QUALITIES MAKE A GOOD MENTOR?

The most important characteristic of a good mentor is a willingness to serve as a mentor. A mentor must be willing to oversee the career and development of the mentee through teaching, counseling, providing psychological support, protecting, and at times promoting and sponsoring. Successful mentors must have significant experience in the area in which they are mentoring. They should be considered experts in their field. When choosing a mentor, why would you want to emulate someone who is not the best at what he or she does?

A mentor must be enthusiastic about the mentoring process, understanding that this is not a commitment to take lightly. Good mentors expend significant time and energy on this relationship and therefore should consider whether their busy schedule will allow them time to mentor someone. If they determine that they do have the time to mentor someone, they must become familiar with the steps in an effective mentoring relationship unless they have benefited from a mentoring relationship themselves.

A good mentor also should have an affinity for the person being mentored. Not all mentoring relationships result in friendships, but a mentoring relationship is doomed to failure if the two do not at least have mutual respect and concern for each other's benefit. This is the reason so many organized mentoring programs fail. Pairing mentors and mentees is a hit-or-miss situation. If the pairs do not like or respect one another, the mentoring relationship will not be successful. It could even be detrimental.

Good mentors, too, are good listeners, show appreciation to those around them, honor people's time, are approachable, are consistent, and honor commitments. These characteristics combine to create individuals who desire to help others reach their fullest potential. Just as these attributes are important in a mentor, they are important in the mentee. The old adage, "To have a good friend, you must first be a good friend," can be adapted to this relationship by saying, "To have a good mentor, you must first be a good mentee."

*S*uggestions for a Good Mentoring Relationship

Developing a strong mentoring relationship entails five basic steps.

1. Get to know one another. Most mentoring relationships develop between two people who are relatively unknown to one another. Time spent getting to know the hopes and dreams of each other is time well spent.

2. Develop realistic expectations of what both want from the mentoring relationship. The importance of stated and shared expectations is critical to the success of the relationship. From these stated expectations, develop a set of goals and objectives to guide the relationship.

3. Develop a schedule of meetings and activities you both will take part in. Some suggested activities for a mentoring relationship include attending a lecture on a topic of mutual interest, attending meetings of each other's associations together (the mentee to see what takes place in the mentor's professional association and the mentor to act as a guest speaker for mentee's organization), working together on a project, and sharing a meal together.

4. Set aside time every 3 or 4 months to evaluate the relationship. Discuss the things that have been beneficial and those that need not be repeated. This is a good time to review the goals and objectives you developed in Step 2, to determine if you are making progress.

5. Based on the findings in Step 4, develop and revise your mentoring relationship plan. There is no standard length of time for a mentoring relationship. Therefore, repeat Steps 1 through 5 as long as both individuals wish the formal mentoring relationship to continue.

*B*uilding Your Professional Network

In the book, *The Career Fitness Program* (Sukiennik, Bendat, and Raufman, 2001), the term *network* is used as both a noun and a verb. As a noun, a network is defined as a group of individuals who are connected to and cooperate with one another. As a verb, "to network" is to develop contacts and exchange information with other people for the purposes of developing business or expanding one's career opportunities. The verb form is action-oriented.

You should begin to develop your professional network during your college years and continue through retirement. "Networking" became a buzzword in the 1990s, but it entails more than just being able to name people by name. Successful professional networking is the result of a carefully developed plan and consistent daily attention to that plan.

A successful professional network also is a two-way street. Although the motivation for developing a network is somewhat self-centered, it requires giving something back. Just as a mentoring relationship must involve give-and-take, so should networking relationships. People will be more willing to assist you in your networking activities if they realize that you are willing to assist them in their goals and objectives as well.

Before you embark on a professional networking plan, you should assess your current relationships to ascertain the extent to which you have already established a network. Many people overlook the reality that they have spent most of their life networking. Make a list of people with whom you currently are in close interaction. These people might be roomate(s), people who live in your residence hall, apartment complex, or housing development, family members, friends you have made in college. Next list people with whom you have less intimate relationships. These might be classmates, professors, people with whom you commute to campus, people with whom you work. Finally, list people with whom you have less contact but who have some impact on your life, such as college or university administrators and employers.

Having assessed your current relationships, develop a vision for your network. What goals do you have for your professional life? What people will you need to help you meet those goals? Develop a list of goals and objectives for your network.

Now look carefully at your own personal qualities. Do you have a healthy outlook on your chosen career? Do you realize that everything that happens in your career begins with you? Do you recognize that you can control a great deal of your professional growth by your own actions and decisions? Do you realize that the people with whom you choose to associate, both personally and professionally, will greatly impact your future?

Understanding that you are in control of your future is an empowering realization. Today the world is full of individuals who blame their circumstances on anyone but themselves. Granted, fate plays a bad joke on people in some instances, but for the most part we have great control over our lives, especially our professional lives. Therefore, you must not merely hope you will become successful. You must deliberately plan and cultivate success. This is accomplished in part by choosing those with whom you associate.

If you are not already part of a professional association through a student chapter in your college, start researching the professional associations in your career field. Every career is associated with at least one professional association. Call this association to find out about student memberships. Even if you are within months of graduation, it is not too late to join. Many associations allow student memberships to continue for up to 2 years after graduation. Because this membership usually carries a much reduced membership fee, it will save you money in the long run. Start attending local meetings and become active in the association.

As you start meeting new career contacts, keep meticulous records. Create a file for each professional association you belong to. In this file keep contact information on the association, its leaders, and everyone with whom you have contact. After each meeting or contact you have with professionals in the association, write a brief note indicating how much you appreciated their help or your conversation with them.

Place notes regarding the important contacts you make in a tickler or file-card system that reminds you periodically to send a note just to keep the relationship fresh. A good way to keep your name in front of people is to keep a record of their specific interests and send them articles that might be of interest to them, along with a brief note. This is a great networking practice. A sample file card is shown in Figure 9.1.

Sample networking file card.

9.1

FIGURE

DR. HENRY J. ROBERTSON   Robertson@pinemail.com

1234 Elm Street

Clinton, MA 12234   Wife: Janet

802-123-1234   Children: James (14)
                                    and Sarah (12)

Interests: Stocks and Bonds
            NASCAR

Also, rely on your mentor to help establish your professional network. Ask the mentor to include you in professional association meetings. Offer to work the registration table so you meet people attending the meeting. Offer to take minutes or to serve in some capacity that will enable you to meet more people.

You may not be in a position to assume a leadership position, but because associations are volunteer organizations, they always need people to help with specific tasks. A word of caution is necessary here: Do not take on more than you can handle with an association, because associations can become a tremendous drain on your resources and hinder your career.

Making Your Network Work for You

In her book *Turning Points,* Diane Ducat (1999) suggests seven ways by which your professional network can assist you. A carefully developed professional network provides:

- experts from whom you can seek advice.
- a guide to assist you in learning new skills or tasks.
- access to people who are "in the know" within your professional community.
- someone to give solace during difficult times in your life.
- someone to motivate you.
- someone who will give you honest, truthful advice.
- necessary introductions to enable you to grow professionally.

Understanding the results you wish to obtain from a professional network in the early stages of developing your professional network will enable you to cultivate a network that is well-rounded and productive.

Networking Skills

Probably the most important networking skill you will need is the ability to meet new people. Develop a comfort level in meeting new people by starting with friends who have contacts that would be good for your network. Ask your friends to make the necessary introductions. Once you've been introduced, develop a relationship with the individual through correspondence or activities, such as notes, articles of shared interest, phone calls, and lunches. Every person you meet and every event you attend provides an opportunity to expand your network.

Another networking skill you must acquire is note-writing. Become a prolific writer. When you meet people, always follow up with a note saying how nice it was to make their acquaintance, and include a business card in the correspondence so they have all of your correct contact information. After phone calls in which you have discussed something of importance that may have to be restated or clarified, follow-up notecards are a good idea. Notes attached to articles of interest to someone in your network will keep your name in front of the person.

Thank-you notes are an essential form of correspondence in a network. Whenever people go out of their way to help you in any way, respond with a thank-you card or note. When selecting your professional stationery, include small notecards that you can use for these occasions. Printed "thank-you" cards are inappropriate for professional correspondence.

Finally, always be on the look-out for ways in which you can be of service to those in your network. Successful networking must be a two-way relationship. Offer to assist those in your network with activities associated with professional associations, charity events, informal work events, and the like. Although you may not have the knowledge or contacts to bring to a networking relationship, you do have a valuable commodity in the form of your time.

References

DiMarco, C. (1997). *Career Transitions: A Journey of Survival and Growth.* Upper Saddle River, NJ: Prentice Hall.

Ducat, D. (1999). *Turning Points: The Career Guide for the New Century.* Upper Saddle River, NJ: Prentice Hall.

Elman, Leslie Gilbert. (1998). Mentoring: Quality Connections. *The Meeting Professional,* October.

Hayes, K. (1996). *Managing Career Transitions: Your Career as a Work in Progress.* Upper Saddle River, NJ: Prentice Hall.

Redfield, James. (1993). *The Celestine Prophecy: An Adventure.* New York: Warner Books.

Rowland, M. (1999). Multiple Mentors. *U.S. AIR Magazine,* April.

Sukiennik, D., Bendat, W., and Raufman, L. (2001). *The Career Fitness Program: Exercising your Options* (6th ed.). Upper Saddle River, NJ: Prentice Hall.

ΛPSTONΣS
FOR NETWORKING

A person can have many
mentors throughout life.

▲

Mentoring is a two-way street.

▲

Mentors should be chosen for their excellence
in what they do.

▲

Mentoring relationships don't "just happen." They must
be built over time.

▲

Mentors should be enthusiastic, willing to share and spend time
with you, and good listeners.

▲

Developing a strong, supportive personal and professional network
requires work, and mentees have to make an effort to stay in close
contact with mentors and networking partners.

Managing Committees and Meetings

Nothing more effectively involves people, sustains creditability, or generates enthusiasm than face-to-face communication.

DANA CORPORATION PHILOSOPHY

A s you move into your career, a great deal of your time will be spent in meetings and with committees. Therefore, you must understand how to make meetings productive and how to ensure that the committees on which you serve are effective. In this chapter we will look at:

▲ Why committees and meetings are important

▲ Preparing to serve on committees

▲ Preparing to participate in meetings

▲ Preparing to chair a committee

▲ How to conduct a meeting and live to tell about it

▲ Meeting minutes

▲ The 6-month rule

▲ Asking thought-provoking questions

Your ability to be productive in meetings and on committees is a crucial element in your promotability. Graduates who understand the importance of their performance on committees and in meetings have reported a significantly higher success rate in promotions and raises. Managing yourself in meetings and on committees therefore will translate into an accelerated career.

Why Committees and Meetings Are Important

No one really knows how many hours are actually spent in meetings each year. A recent survey of 2,000 business leaders indicated that managers are spending more time in meetings than years ago. Some managers estimate 70 percent of their average day is spent in meetings. That figure does not include hours used preparing for meetings, analyzing the results of meetings, and scheduling new meetings. All this occurs in spite of the fact that the same study indicated that managers felt that about one-third of those meetings are unproductive, leading to an estimated $37 billion a year in wasted time. (Burleson, 1990, p. 1)

Why, then, do meetings continue to be conducted? Why are people continuously being appointed to committees that must hold meetings? Generally, companies use committees and meetings because *effective* committees and their meetings:

- do most of the work in a company.
- enable the company to benefit from the expertise of a variety of staff members on a project that spans departments and areas.
- increase the lines of communication throughout the company.
- enable open discussion of important issues.
- provide opportunities for younger associates in a company to become active in the company's decision-making process.
- equip individuals to improve their management skills and thereby prepare them for future promotions.
- serve as vehicles to solve problems and make decisions.

Although many managers and executives see committees as something that "keep minutes and waste hours," effective committees can enable an organization to compete more successfully in today's competitive world. The old saying that two minds are better than one is accurate. The key is in making these committees and their subsequent meetings productive.

Preparing to Serve on Committees

You generally will not have a say in serving on committees and attending meetings. You usually are assigned to committees or directed to attend certain meetings. Irrespective of whether you are interested in the committee or meeting to which you are assigned, you must prepare thoroughly, ensuring that you bring your best efforts to the table. When you are appointed to a committee, ask yourself the following questions:

1. Am I familiar with the mission and goals of the committee or meeting? If the answer is no, call the person responsible for chairing the meeting and ask him or her to provide you an overview of the mission and goals. If it is an existing committee, ask for a review of past minutes from previous meetings.

2. Having read the information, do I understand the mission and goals? Am I prepared to share factual information with the others on the com-

mittee or attending the meeting? If the answer is no, do research on the topic to enable you to be an informed participant on the committee or in the meeting. Specifically know what your department is responsible for in accomplishing the mission of the committee or meeting.

3. Do I understand my superior's position on the mission and goals of the committee or meeting? If the answer is no, schedule a meeting with your boss prior to the committee or meeting to ask for insights into the mission and goals of the committee or meeting.

4. Am I familiar with the other committee members or participants? If the answer is no, ask your committee chair so you are not clueless when sitting at the table with them. Suggest that the committee chair make brief introductions so you can begin to put names with faces. Committees represent an excellent opportunity for you to begin developing your internal network.

Preparing to Participate in Meetings

Prior to attending a first meeting, prepare yourself for the meeting in the following ways.

1. Develop a folder with the title of the committee and the contact information for the chair on the cover. Use color folders so you can color-code the different committees and areas of your job to enable you to quickly identify what you need if you are running late to a meeting.

   We also suggest that you use folders with the clasp at the top of both sides. These folders enable you to attach your minutes and handouts so you can keep accurate notes on the committee's work. On the left side of the folder cover, you could place lined paper upon which to take notes. On the right side of the folder cover, you can attach handouts from the meetings. Keep the attachments in chronological order, labeling the most important items with stick-on tabs for easy access.

2. Scan previous minutes and notes you developed during your preparation for serving on the committee.

3. Bring all necessary supplies to the meeting (writing utensil, paper, your personal planner, paperclips, a highlighter).

   During the meeting you should:

1. Take good notes, highlighting any items that require your action.

2. Participate in the meeting when you have information or facts that are relevant.

3. Be prepared to ask thought-provoking questions to enable your committee to carefully think-through critical decisions.

4. Practice the two-to-one principle: Listen twice as much as you speak.

5. Don't commit your department to something over which you do not have authority. If asked for a commitment, say that you must discuss it with your superior and that you will get back to them.

6. Adhere to meeting manners and established protocol.

    a. Arrive between 5 and 10 minutes prior to the meeting so you can organize yourself.

    b. Never smoke in a meeting. It may negatively impact your image.

    c. If refreshments are served, choose only items that you can eat inconspicuously, and don't speak with your mouth full. Avoid items that tend to stick in your teeth to avoid embarrassing yourself. Beverages tend to sweat, so place a coaster or napkin under your beverage to avoid a pool of condensation at your place.

    d. Choose your seating carefully. The seat directly to the right of the chair usually is reserved for the next-in-command. Make sure you can hear all participants. (Hint: Do not sit beside people who tend to chatter—even if they are friends. Talking to people during a meeting about unrelated information or sharing inside jokes is rude and may have a negative impact on your career.)

    e. Never use profanity or inappropriate language or make improper jokes.

    f. If your schedule dictates that you have to leave a meeting early, inform the chair prior to the meeting. Leave as quietly as possible so you do not disrupt the flow of conversation. Call the committee chair later in the day to find out what you missed.

    g. Leave your seat and work area as free of debris as you found it. The committee chair is not your mother and, therefore, should not be expected to clean up after you.

After the meeting:

1. Carefully read through your notes to ensure that you understand them. Transfer all highlighted items you must act upon to your planner so that they become a part of your "To Do" plan. Develop an action plan that enables you to complete your task prior to the next meeting.

2. Provide an overview of the meeting for your superior, either in writing, through email, or through a meeting. We suggest that whenever you have a meeting with your superior about significant issues, you follow up in writing to ensure that you both understand what transpired during the meeting.

Preparing to Chair a Committee

If you are appointed, elected, or volunteered to serve as chair for a committee, you should take several preparatory steps to ensure that you and your committee are effective. At the foundation of your committee should be a clearly defined and communicated mission statement and goals and objectives for the committee. This mission statement coupled with the committee goals and objectives should be communicated verbally and in writing to all committee members to assure that everyone is working from the same page. If you have the option of choosing your committee members, select them carefully. Pick individuals who are familiar with the areas affected by the actions of the committee, are able to express themselves easily and clearly, have a cooperative nature, are willing to give of their time and energy to fulfill the committee mission, and have expertise that the committee requires to complete its task. A primary duty of the committee chair is to keep the committee

ΛDVIC∑ FROM Λ M∑NTOR

Charles A. Goodwin,

General Manager
Jefferson Lakeside Country Club,
Richmond, VA

On any given day, I work with the chairman of the board, board members, committee members, club members, and staff members. Much of this interaction takes place in the form of meetings. Because of the large amount of my time spent in meetings, I must ensure that the time I work with committees and attend meetings is productive for both myself and the other participants.

My interpersonal skills are my strongest asset. Years ago, I learned how to put people at ease, help them relax, ask the right questions and, most important, I learned how to listen. While attending committee meetings, I find my most important function is to listen to what the others are saying. When I know what people need and want, I am able to create an environment where they feel comfortable and enjoy working.

I would challenge you to take the time to polish your communication, listening, and interpersonal skills while in school, or focused and motivated to complete the mission. To do this, committee chairs cannot take on many of the committee tasks themselves. They must use their energies to move the committee forward—something they would be unable to do if they had to focus on smaller issues. A committee chair also should be responsible for following up with committee members prior to the meetings to confirm that members are working on their assignments.

Finally, a committee chair is responsible for recognizing committee members and rewarding them for their efforts. Recognition could come in several forms—including all the names of committee members on the final report, introducing the committee members to the entire organization and thanking them publicly, writing letters to committee members' immediate supervisor expressing your gratitude for their participation on the committee.

Most committees are not volunteer committees and, therefore, are part of a job description. Consequently, they normally don't have monetary rewards. If the committee members have participated above and beyond the call of duty, however, you may wish to give small tokens of your appreciation accompanied by a letter expressing your gratitude. The committee member should place this letter in his or her career portfolio and use it during the annual evaluation process.

ow to Conduct a Meeting and Live To Tell About It

A poorly planned and conducted meeting is the main downfall of committees. If you are chairing the committee or directing the proposed meeting you should ask yourself a series of questions to assist you in deciding whether to hold the meeting.

1. Do I need the group to accomplish the task, or is this something I could handle by phone with a few key people?

2. Will a meeting save time by allowing us to accomplish more faster?

3. Do I need the group to meet to allow me to gain their commitment?

4. Do I have everything I need to conduct this meeting properly (time, answers to questions, supplies)?

ΛDVIÇΣ
CONTINUED.
once you are out attend professional development workshops focused on these areas. Being an active, empathetic listener has enabled me to find true success in my professional career. Use every opportunity to master the fine art of communication, and you will be light years ahead of your competition in the job market.

5. Do my committee members have the time to meet?

6. Will my committee members have enough time to prepare adequately for the meeting?

If you did not answer yes to any of these questions, you should reconsider holding the meeting and handle the necessary business through another forum.

As you plan for the meeting observe the following steps.

1. Establish meeting goals and objectives.

2. Plan an agenda and disseminate the agenda to your committee members prior to the meeting.

3. Secure meeting space and necessary supplies to ensure that the meeting will run smoothly.

4. Notify committee members of the meeting and inform them of when, what, where, how, and why.

5. Arrive early for the meeting to be sure that everything is ready.

6. Conduct the meeting in an organized manner.

7. Review the decisions and assign specific duties to committee members.

8. Develop an action plan to include due dates.

9. Determine the committee's next meeting time.

10. End the meeting on time.

As soon as possible following the meeting, transcribe the meeting minutes and forward a copy to all committee members. Minutes should include a comprehensive action plan that sets forth an overview of important discussion items, action items, responsible parties, and due dates. These minutes serve as a reminder to your committee members of the tasks they agreed to complete. Using the minutes for your outline you can develop the agenda for the next meeting.

Meeting Minutes

Throughout your career, you may be responsible either for the taking minutes or preparing minutes from a meeting. The book *Effective Meetings: The Complete Guide* (Burleson, 1990) provides an excellent checklist for preparing minutes. Effective minutes include the date of the meeting, time and place of the meeting, who attended the meeting (possibly including the names of those absent), and the body of minutes. The body of minutes should include:

Call to order
Example: *The meeting was called to order at 8:15 a.m. by Jamie Langston.*

Attendees
Example: *In attendance were: (names and titles)*

Those absent
Example: *Absent were: (name and titles)*

Previous minutes read and approved
Example: *The minutes of the previous session were read. Tom Rogers offered an amendment dealing with item 7, the costs reviewed, and this was accepted. The minutes were approved.*

Agenda and opening
Example: *Jamie reviewed the agenda and made a brief opening statement, which included the following facts: (itemized).*

Discussion: Presentation
Example: *The discussion began with Roger Lowery's presentation of the financial aspects of the situation.*

Discussion: Questions
Example: *Jack Brown and Kate Lee asked several questions, including: (listed).*

Discussion: Responses
Example: *Roger responded to their satisfaction, and the group proceeded to discuss the matter.*

Discussion: Facts
Example: *At this point comes coverage of the discussion, including names, positions, and pertinent facts.*

Record of vote
Example: *A vote was taken. The following attendees voted to: (names, recommendations). The following attendees voted against that stance and recommended: (names, recommendations).*

Decision
Example: *The matter was decided as follows: (names, positions, decision).*

Call of unanimity
Example: *Jamie Langston summarized the action of the group and requested that the decision be made unanimous.*

Record of agreement/disagreement

Example: *The group agreed and the decision is unanimous (or Tom Brown, Quincy Wright, and Steve Pilhl disagreed, and the minutes show their continued opposition to the decision).*

Summary

Example: *Jamie recapped the activity and discussion.*

Next meeting

Example: *The group agreed to meet again on February 11, 1990, in the Baxter Conference Room at 9:45 a.m. At that time, the following individuals will present the indicated reports: (names).*

Adjournment

Example: *The meeting was adjourned at 11:55 a.m.*

The amount of detail included in the minutes is subject to the individual's or company's desire. If you are requested to take minutes prior to the meeting, ask to see a copy of the minutes from the last meeting. If this is the first meeting, ask to see a copy of the minutes from another meeting so you can follow the same format. It is best to set up an outline prior to the meeting so you only have to fill in the details during the actual meeting.

Transcribe your minutes as quickly as possible to ensure that you don't forget important details. Before disseminating the minutes, have the committee chair review them to make sure they are correct.

If you are not responsible for taking minutes, it is still good to make your own record—abbreviated, of course—of meetings you attend. These personal minutes can be used to refresh your memory of ideas and concerns about specific issues. Keep your minutes, agendas, and official minutes all in the same file so you can access them readily if necessary. You should keep your files for at least 18 months after the committee has ceased to be. If it is a very important committee, you may want to keep the files much longer.

The 6-Month Rule

If the time you have spent in higher education has been productive, you should leave with a sense of accomplishment. You should leave with basic understanding of your discipline, and you should leave with an understanding of just how much you *do not know*. We are all—and should continue to be—students in life. The aim of higher education is to teach you to become lifelong learners.

Never is it more important for you to be a good student than it is during your first 6 months on a job. Many newly minted graduates have shot themselves in the foot during those first 6 months on the job by acting like they know it all. We strongly suggest that during those first 6 months, you focus more on asking questions than on answering them.

There is much to learn during your first 6 months at a job. You must learn about the company culture, about the business and your clients, about the company's expectations of your work, and about the company politics—to name just a few areas. Preparing for finals is nothing compared to preparing for your career during the first 6 months. You should take copious notes, study every night, and be seen much more than you are heard. "It's better to remain quiet and be thought a fool than to speak and remove all doubt." Carefully weigh what you say. As Irving Shapiro, past Chairman of Du Pont, once said, "People who accomplish things do more listening than talking."

Learn How to Ask Thought-Provoking Questions

Don't confuse asking thought-provoking questions with becoming the Devil's advocate who brings up the negative side of every argument. Rather, learn how to listen and then to ask questions that enable your colleagues to more carefully think-through their plan of action. Listening to your customers, clients, colleagues, and staff is the best way to understand every situation. When he was a junior senator, former President Lyndon B. Johnson had a sign on his door stating, "You ain't learnin' nothin' when you're doing all the talkin'." We suggest you heed his advice.

References

Burleson, Clyde. (1990). *Effective Meetings: The Complete Guide.* New York: John Wiley & Sons.

CAPSTONES

FOR MANAGING COMMITTEES AND MEETINGS

Planning and conducting a meeting entails 10 steps.

▲

Proper meeting etiquette is essential.

▲

Good preparation prior to meetings allows you to bring your best to the table.

▲

After each meeting, time spent organizing your notes will be helpful later.

▲

Research on committees and meetings requires that you know the mission, goals, and objectives prior to attending your first meeting.

▲

You should understand your role as committee chair before accepting the assignment or nomination.

▲

The 6-month rule requires you to listen and learn more than you talk during the first 6 months on your first job.

CHAPTER 11

Resolving Conflicts and Working with Difficult People

If you are patient in one moment of anger, you will save yourself a hundred days of sorrow.

CHINESE PROVERB

W e've all felt it before. It creeps up on us like the flu. We never expected it to happen, but before we know it, in a moment of anger, during a misunderstanding, dealing with a difficult colleague, or in a jealous rage, we lose control. In a heated moment of emotional turmoil, we say things or do something that causes conflict and serious problems at work or at home. As a consequence, relationships are damaged, friends and colleagues are hurt, and we gain the reputation of being a "hothead." Could a moment of patience have prevented the conflict? Could knowing how to control our emotions have prevented the situation? If we understood the causes of conflict, could we have avoided the unpleasantness?

The word "conflict" comes from the Latin, *conflictus,* meaning "striking together with force" (Johnson & Johnson, 1994). Conflict has many causes as there are people in the world. What causes one person to go off the deep end may only slightly irritate another person. Because resolving conflict and dealing with difficult people are two immensely important skills needed in today's workplace, this chapter will discuss the following topics:

▲ Myths about conflict

▲ A definition of conflict resolution

▲ Seven dragons of conflict

     failing to consider the individual

     idea killing

     unclear jurisdiction

     constant change

     interpersonal incompatibility

     assumptions

     harsh criticism

▲ Resolving conflict

▲ Learning from conflict

Myths About Conflict

Conflict can happen between anyone, even the very best of friends. If there is not some type of conflict, the relationship is more than likely stale, lifeless, and insignificant. Often we assume that all conflict is bad, when in reality some conflict can be healthy. "Conflict is a normal part of life. Disagreements actually help us grow" (Donahue, 1998).

Consider the following statements outlined by Joseph DeVito (1993) concerning conflict:

- If two people in a relationship fight, it means their relationship is a bad one.
- Fighting hurts an interpersonal relationship.
- Fighting is bad because it reveals your negative self—for example, your pettiness, your need to be in control, or your unreasonable expectations.

If you think these statements are true, you are correct. If you think they are false, you are also correct. The three assumptions may all be true or false (DeVito, 1993). For some conflicts, each of these myths or statements may very well be true. Relationships may be damaged and friends lost. For some people, though, a verbal argument may be just what was needed to clear the air and move on.

Clearly, conflict can have a positive or a negative impact. The outcome depends on the people involved. Some of the *negative aspects* of conflict are:

Seriously hurt feelings

Negative statements unfairly brought into the discussion

One or more parties turning away and refusing to negotiate, thereby extending the conflict

People who normally would not team together now forming an alliance against others

Statements made in the heat of the moment that never will be forgotten or forgiven

Stress, anger, discomfort, and tension among colleagues

Some of the *positive aspects* of conflict are:

As a result of being forced to work through a situation, making the relationship stronger and more viable

Clearing the air

Causing people to examine situations and develop new strategies or solutions, leading to growth and progression

Helping people get what they want

Reducing resentment through conflict resolution

Helping you understand how others feel

Expanding communication

Another positive aspect of conflict that can be managed properly is the reduction of stress. In a study conducted by the University of Wisconsin–Madison, an investigation was conducted on "how surviving middle managers from downsized organizations handle stressors related to organizational changes" (Antonioni, 1995). The study found that managers who engaged in conflict management had significantly lower stress levels than managers who did not.

If we learn to deal with conflict positively, we can gain much success in the workplace. One of the most important gains that can be made through conflict, according to DeVito (1993), is that if two or more people resolve a conflict, they have, in essence, made the decision that the relationship was worth saving. This, too, is a positive aspect of conflict.

What Is Conflict Resolution?

Conflict resolution may not be what you think it is. It is not, all together, getting what you want. It also is not giving up all that you need.

> Conflict resolution is a way to settle disagreements peacefully by getting to the root of problems and finding solutions. It is working things out without violence, name calling, or hurting the feelings of others, without running away from difficult situations or going against your feelings or beliefs. (Channing L. Bete Co., 1996)

Some conflicts are easily resolved, and others can take weeks or months. To more effectively resolve conflicts personally and professionally, you should first understand some of the major causes of conflict in today's world.

Seven Dragons of Conflict

Just as you never know when the flu is going to strike, you never really know what or who will cause conflict within your workplace. Even the best laid plans and the most compassionate thought given to detail will not please some people. Sadly, but realistically, conflict inevitably will arise. Nevertheless, whether you are working at or below the management level, you can do things to either cause or avert conflict.

Below are some of the most common ways to *cause conflict* and unrest. Use them and watch the sparks begin to fly!

▲ ▲ ▲

DRAGON 1: FAILING TO CONSIDER THE INDIVIDUAL

The first dragon of conflict is when you, the company, or the management does not consider the individual. So many people do not consider the issue of diversity when making decisions and changes. Conflict can arise when we fail to understand the differences in culture, age, sex, race, religion, ideals, history, sexual orientation, values, and family. No one can please 100 percent of the people 100 percent of the time. Much conflict can be avoided, however, simply by asking questions and recognizing that we work in a multifaceted environment with people who have varied lifestyles, personalities, and responsibilities. We may think that a simple decision will not impact anyone negatively, but we should consider daily the feelings of individuals who share their talents and expertise with us. Effective conflict managers know that, to achieve the good of the whole, the individual pieces must be considered at some point.

▲ ▲ ▲

DRAGON 2: IDEA KILLING

If you want to cause more conflict than you can imagine, begin the meeting or the planning retreat with the dragon of idea killing. This happens when employees or colleagues are asked for their opinions and their ideas, and, regardless of how creative or unrealistic, the ideas are, they are "killed" on the spot. Conflict arises because they do not feel that their voice counts. Often an employee will come to the company with a new way of doing something, a fresh approach developed by working in the field every day. Immediately, the approach is scoffed at because it came from a person "below" management or because the person was never asked to *think*, only to *do*.

Excellent mangers and employees know the value in the advice of people who are "in the trenches" every day. They seek solutions from the people who know the process. Idea killing muffles any desire for an employee to add to the well-being of the company.

▲ ▲ ▲

DRAGON 3: UNCLEAR JURISDICTION

Unclear jurisdiction and overlapping functions will unleash the third dragon of conflict. A hotel employee was heard complaining and commiserating with another employee. It seems as if they had spent the day doing the same task. They did not know this to begin with, but as they talked and shared their frustrations, they began to realize that the reason neither could accomplish the task fully was that the other one had the information needed to complete the project. After this discussion, they decided to approach their supervisor, who told them that he had assigned them the same task to see who could complete it first. Just think of the manpower and energy wasted and the frustration this caused! In this instance, conflict was precipitated by poor leadership.

As you begin your profession and specific job, you should have a clear understanding of your job description. If you do not know, you should ask immediately. If you are in a supervisory role, you should empower your team members with the tools, knowledge, and technology to

Advice from a Mentor

Larry Joe Perdue, CCM, CHE

Academic Advisor

Club Managers Association of America,

Alexandria, VA

I don't know of one profession, job, or organization where conflict has not happened. It is inevitable that people may not get along, problems may arise, misunderstandings will happen, and personalities will clash. In my profession of hospitality, I have seen conflict cause insurmountable problems and I have seen conflict make an organization or a team stronger.

I think the difference between the two situations has been open communication and effective negotiation skills. These two skills are essential in today's office. If people let problems go unattended, they will only fester. However, if people come together with an

open mind and a willingness to give and share, most problems and conflicts can be resolved. It is only when people are unwavering that conflict grows.

The advice that I would give to you as you enter the world of work is this: Don't allow one negative event, situation, or person get in your way or destroy your long-range goals. There will always be make the job happen. Your team members should know that they are trusted and that management is not out to sabotage them. Failing to communicate or facilitate these elements will certainly cause conflict.

▲ ▲ ▲

DRAGON 4: CREATING CONSTANT, UNNECESSARY CHANGE

Although change is necessary in any venue, stability is also appreciated. Change for change's sake is dangerous, and employees usually have to suffer the consequences. New technology and innovations have been introduced in the past few years that have made almost every company, industry, and educational institution more competitive and cost-productive. This is good, but it also has come at a price. Realizing that some things work well as they are and should stay the same can reduce the amount of conflict caused by constant and unneeded change.

▲ ▲ ▲

DRAGON 5: INTERPERSONAL INCOMPATIBILITY

Regardless of how much you try, how much you listen, how many ideas you accept, how clearly you state job descriptions, and how strongly you consider the individuals involved, from time to time there is going to be interpersonal incompatibility. To ignore this reality as a conflict manager would be a huge miscalculation. Any interpersonal situation has countless components—race, gender, sexual orientation, culture, age, religion, and values, to name but a few.

Many times, interpersonal incompatibility arises between two or more people because of differences that have not been addressed on any level. The conflict might arise because neither party is willing to try to understand the other party.

Interpersonal communication is complex. It is "communication that exists when two or more people are in a relationship" (DeVito, 1993). This relationship does not have to be as friends, lovers, or family members. The relationship also can be a "working relationship." In that light, issues such as roles, self-concept, emotions, social comparisons, image, perception, abilities, ethics, competence, desire, and fear come into play.

ΛDVI¢Σ
CONTINUED.
conflict, there will always be people who try to get in your way and hinder you from reaching your goals, but you must learn to live above them. Take the high road and don't get involved in petty gossip, office rumors, or politics that don't affect you. Remember, the best revenge is a life well-lived.

Resolving interpersonal conflict requires negotiation. The challenge of negotiation, according to David Johnson (1993), is considering that both parties have needs and wants.

> To meet his/her needs and wants, each person makes proposals to others. The other persons evaluate the proposal on the basis of how well it meets their needs and wants and either agrees to make a counter-proposal. Negotiation is a process by which persons who have shared and opposed interests want to come to an agreement and try to work out a settlement.

When working to resolve interpersonal conflict and incompatibility, your duty is to discover means by which all parties will benefit. This is much easier said than done. It is easier said than done when it involves working with things or jobs. Working with people is a different situation altogether. When working-through the conflict, Johnson suggests, you can do several things to assist in overcoming and moving beyond the situation:

- Do not withdraw from or ignore the conflict.
- Do not engage in win-lose negotiations.
- Assess for smoothing possibilities.
- When the time is short, compromise.
- Initiate problem-solving negotiations.
- Use your sense of humor.

As a negotiator in interpersonal conflict and incompatibility, you can do much to assist the parties involved in reaching a mutually desirable end. You can't change them, but you can help them see the grander picture. You can help them move beyond, "I need," "I want," I demand," "I feel that," and "If I don't get what I want, I'll . . . ." You must try to create an atmosphere where agreement can be visualized. Johnson (1993) calls it an "Agreement Menu."

- Meet in the middle.
- Take turns.
- Share.
- Let chance decide.
- Create a package deal in which several issues are considered and discussed.
- Trade off (exchange two things of equal value).
- Tie-in extraneous issues offered by the opposing party.
- Carve-out issues from a larger context, leaving the related issue unsettled.

▲ ▲ ▲

DRAGON 6: ASSUMING THAT EVERYONE HAS THE SAME ASSUMPTION

"Assuming" is a dangerous word. It suggests a lack of communication and a lack of leadership. Conflict managers should not assume that the message is clear, that the word is out, that the job is done, or that Jane and John get along. To make an assumption means that you have not done the research to determine the truth.

Many conflicting situations can be avoided simply by telling the truth so each employee has the same information. Managers should not assume that everyone is singing from the same page of a songbook even if everyone has the same songbook. Conflict managers must go beyond simply handing out information and supplying technology that make information more accessible. We must move back to human-touch communication and asking questions, probing for answers, talking about solutions, and verbally testing for comprehension.

To simply put an employee handbook in employees' possession does not mean they have read or understand the information. Making that assumption will result in conflict when the employee performs a function improperly and then suggests that he or she did not know any better.

▲ ▲ ▲

DRAGON 7: HARSH CRITICISM AND LACK OF FEEDBACK

Constructive criticism and directed feedback are two tools that can assist the conflict manager in creating and maintaining harmony. Constructive criticism may not eliminate conflict, but harsh criticism and lack of feedback or inappropriate feedback will cause conflict every time.

Lack of feedback can cause as much conflict as harsh or inappropriate feedback. Our days are busy, and we struggle sometimes just trying to accomplish the tasks at hand. Seldom do we schedule time for feedback sessions, positive and negative. Harsh criticism serves only two purposes: isolation and contempt. Both breed infectious conflict.

Managers should arrange times weekly to meet with employees to discuss progress, problems, concerns, and conflicts. They should make a concerted effort to mail letters, cards, notes, and personal comments not only to employees who perform extraordinarily but also to those who perform their required duties in a professional manner. Praise and constructive feedback serve as a monumental motivator to most people.

Giving constructive criticism and feedback is an art. Different types of criticism and feedback elicit varying responses. For the most part, non-threatening, positive feedback and criticism will meet with little resistance. This depends, of course, on the self-image of the person giving *and* receiving the criticism and the art by which the criticism is given. Some hints for constructive criticism are as follows (Brownell, 1996):

Is the feedback descriptive, not evaluative? Descriptive feedback gives direction. It does not just state whether some behavior was good or bad, but goes farther in giving details of how something was good or bad.

Positive:

"Jane, that was one of the best catering jobs I've ever seen. The food was wonderful, the flowers were perfect, the setting was classy, and the staff gave excellent service."

Constructive:

"Jane, the catering job for the James's party was good. The food was wonderful, and the flowers were perfect. Next week, however, you'll need to have maintenance people lower the lights and you'll need to talk with your serving staff about the clanging dishes and loud noises in the back."

Negative/Attacking:

"I can't imagine what you were thinking about by having those lights so bright and why weren't you there to tell your staff to stop clanging those dishes?"

Does the criticism focus on the behavior, not on personal characteristics? Is it specific? Focused criticism should begin in the first person: "I feel," "I believe," "I have found that . . . ."

Positive:

"Tim, I think you did a fine job on that budget report. President Andros was very pleased, as was I."

Constructive:

"Tim, I believe the budget report looked good. There was only one area where we needed some clarification. If you were to show us the room yield report in a chart, it would be very helpful."

Negative/Attacking:

"Tim, if you weren't so careless and spent more time on your projects and not in the employee lounge, you might have been able to write a more impressive budget report."

Is the feedback timed appropriately? If you are angry, you should wait until you have cooled off before approaching the situation. But you shouldn't wait until the next week. That's too late.

Positive:

"Tina, let's get together at four o'clock today to talk about your work on the front-desk project."

Constructive:

"Tina, there are a few things that I would like to discuss with you about improving the front-desk project. Let's meet at four o'clock in my office."

Negative/Attacking:

"Tina, we've never talked about this before, but you didn't do a very good job on that last front-desk project. We need to get together sometime to talk about what went wrong so you won't make the same mistakes again."

Is the feedback offered, not imposed? Most people welcome feedback and constructive criticism. To make the most out of the situation, always offer, never impose criticism or feedback.

Positive:

"Alex, I would like to talk with you about some ideas for the upcoming conference at the hotel. Do you want to get together tomorrow for lunch and talk about it?"

Constructive:

"Alex, I helped arrange this conference a few years ago and learned a lot about what has to be done on the floor. Would you like to get together for lunch tomorrow and talk about it?"

Negative/Attacking:

"Alex, I need to talk to you about this upcoming conference and the plans you have. We can't afford to have you and your staff ill-prepared on this one."

Communication experts such as DeVito (1993, 1995), Adler (1989), Brownell (1996), Johnson (1993), and Cohen (1994) have conducted much research regarding the best way to give constructive feedback and criticism. A synopsis is presented below for your consideration as a conflict manager:

- State criticism and feedback positively.
- Treat disagreements objectively.
- Don't attack the person; deal with the action.
- Reaffirm the other person's sense of competence.
- Own your own words. Be direct, and use the first person, such as, "I think . . . ."

- State your concern for the other person and his or her well-being.
- Don't ask someone to read your mind; be specific about the praise or criticism.
- Avoid interrupting; allow the other person to complete his or her side.
- Don't become overly emotional.
- Be honest but not cruel.
- Allow the other person to save face; don't use humiliation as a tactic.
- Try to end the feedback/criticism session on a positive note.

Resolving Conflict

For the number of people who can cause conflict and the number of conflicts as there can be in the world of work, there are just as many solutions. Most conflict managers and resolution experts, however, suggest using a format that contains some, if not all, of the following steps:

1. Define the conflict. Get to the root of problems, not just the symptoms.
2. Talk about your feelings and emotions, and let others involved talk about theirs.
3. Develop solutions to the conflict in which all involved have input.
4. Generate a list of alternative solutions as backup, if needed.
5. Implement the first list of solutions, in which everyone has ownership.
6. Evaluate the solutions to determine if they worked.
7. If the solutions worked, you should be out of the conflict. If they did not work, implement one of your alternative solutions.

Learning From Conflict

Effective conflict managers "learn from the conflict and the process they went through" (DeVito, 1995). To learn as much as possible from the conflict, DeVito suggests that conflict managers ask themselves the following questions:

- Can you identify the fight strategies that aggravated the situation?
- Was a cooling off period needed?
- Can you now determine if major issues will turn into major disagreements?

- Did avoidance make matters worse?
- What were the issues that started the conflict?
- Can these issues be avoided?

As a conflict manager, keep the conflict in perspective. Try to reflect on past experiences: Has this happened before? If so, how was it handled then? Was the solution effective? Don't become negative, and don't assume the situation is hopeless. Although not all conflicts can be resolved, keeping your feelings in check will assist you in helping others overcome or move beyond interpersonal incompatibility and resolve conflicts.

References

Adler, R., et al. (1989). *Interplay: The Process of Interpersonal Communication* (4th ed.). New York: Holt, Rinehart and Winston.

Antonioni, D. (1995) Practicing Conflict Management Can Reduce Organizational Stress. *Industrial Management*, Sept.–Oct., Vol. 37, No. 5, p. 7.

Brownell, Judi. (1996). *Listening: Attitudes, Principles and Skills*. Boston: Allyn and Bacon.

Cohen, R. (1994). *Psychology and Adjustment: Values, Culture, and Change*. Boston: Allyn and Bacon.

Channing L. Bete Co. (1996). *Successful Conflict Resolution: A Skill for Working Together*. Chicago, IL: Channing L. Bete Co.

DeVito, J. (1993). *Messages: Building Interpersonal Communication Skills*. New York: HarperCollins College Publishers.

DeVito, J. (1995). *The Interpersonal Communication Handbook* (7th ed.). New York: HarperCollins College Publisher.

Donahue, M. (1998). Let's Negotiate! *Current Health*, February, Vol. 24, No. 6, p. 13.

Johnson, D. (1993). *Reaching Out: Interpersonal Effectiveness and Self-actualization* (5th ed.). Boston: Allyn and Bacon.

Johnson, D., and Johnson, F. (1994). *Joining Together: Group Theory and Group Skills*. Boston: Allyn and Bacon.

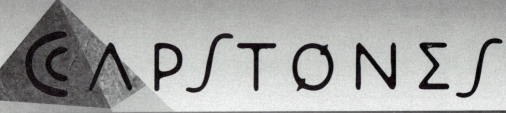

CAPSTONES

FOR RESOLVING CONFLICT

Interpersonal incompatibility
is a factor in conflict.

▲

Much conflict can be prevented by
being truthful and upfront.

▲

When making decisions, managers have to consider the individual people involved.

▲

All conflict is not bad. Some conflict actually promotes growth.

▲

Conflict managers should allow others to give their ideas and opinions.

▲

Managers should avoid unnecessary change or turmoil just for the sake of
change.

▲

Assumptions can be eliminated by holding meetings, writing reports to everyone, and having a newsletter or other information-sharing ventures.

▲

Managers should strive to make sure that everyone knows his or her jurisdiction.

▲

Conflict managers should give as much constructive and positive feedback
as possible.

Discovering the Leader in You

Whoever heard of a world manager? World leader? . . . yes. Educational leader, political leader, religious leader, scout leader, community leader, labor leader, business leader. . . . They lead; they don't manage. The carrot wins over the stick. Ask your horse—you can lead your horse to water, but you can't manage him to drink.

UNITED TECHNOLOGIES

$\int$ ylvia managed a small business with 57 employees. The company sold kitchen supplies to major hotels around the country. Many of the contacts and transactions involved the use of technology such as the Internet, email, FedEx, online tracking, and faxes. Sylvia provided her employees the finest computers and telephone systems available. Division managers constantly studied and evaluated the latest technology and if it was determined to be necessary, it was supplied to field employees.

Because the company had invested so much time, effort, and resources in technology, Sylvia expected to see a vast improvement in the sales figures from the last three quarters. To her dismay, this quarter looked as dismal as last year. "Why was this so?" she questioned herself. What else do they need? How much more can I and the division managers do to improve sales?

Sylvia could not put her finger on the problem, so she decided to call a company meeting to discuss future strategies and how to use technology to increase sales. Shortly after the meeting began, she asked questions about the company's vision and philosophy. She randomly went around the room and asked, "Where is this company going to be in five years or ten years?" "What is our role in the hospitality industry?" Few members of the sales staff had the answers for which Sylvia was looking. Finally she asked the question, "What else do you need from me to help you do your jobs to get our profits up?"

At first there was silence. Finally, a lone sales member answered, "We need to know where you're going. We need to know what you want from us. We need for you to lead us, not manage us."

Sylvia was speechless for a moment as the flood of responses started coming. She listened to sales member after sales member echo the same sentiments. Until that moment, Sylvia thought she had been leading. She thought all of the technology and training that she and the division managers offered was sufficient. What she had failed to realize is that no amount of technology, no computer, no fax, and no Internet connection can ever replace the power of human leadership. As a manager, she had provided the staff with world-class gadgets, but as a leader, she had failed to provide a vision. She had not built a team. She had not addressed problems and conflicts that human beings encounter. In short, Sylvia had not addressed the human side of leading humans.

Because your new career may—and probably will—require you to assume leadership positions, this chapter will discuss:

▲ Management versus leadership

▲ Power versus force

▲ Categories of leadership power

▲ The human touch of leadership

▲ 10 basic qualities of remarkable leaders

▲ 12 results of leadership

Manager Versus Leader

Knowing the difference between managing and leading is "critical to becoming an enlightened leader; it ranks second only to self-knowledge among our six principles of leadership" (McLean and Weitzel, 1992). Some adjectives commonly associated with managing and leading are:

MANAGEMENT	LEADERSHIP
Restricting	Enabling
Controlling	Freeing
Playing safe	Risking
Molding	Releasing
Forcing	Enhancing
Stifling	Participating
Rigid	Flexible
Consistent	Predictable

This list sums up the old adage, "You manage things; you lead people." If you think about the two words in motivational terms, would you want to be managed or led? The word "manage" has connotations that can create negative feelings from the onset. Many view the word as synonymous with manipulate.

In a thesaurus, you will find the words *administer, direct, oversee, control, maneuver,* and *handle* associated with the word *manage.* If you look at the same source for the word "leader," you will find terms such as *guide, influence, pacesetter, explorer,* and *pioneer.*

Managers seem to need more control and are more structured in their desire to accomplish a task. They usually give directions more than they ask for help. Leaders, in contrast, tend to be more flexible and less structured. They do not give orders as much as they ask for assistance and input. In human terms, managers are more concerned with how the body functions and leaders are more concerned with how the soul feels.

Power Versus Force

Power is a strange thing. So many people seek it, yet few achieve lasting, meaningful power. Abraham Lincoln once remarked, "Nearly all people can stand adversity, but if you want to test their true character, give them power." Many people confuse management with leadership, just as many confuse power with force.

The strangest thing about power is that the less of it you use, the more you seem to have. It is like a precious commodity that few people know how to use. The weakest leaders are those who use their power for trivial reasons or personal gain. They race through the office arousing fear and dread because they think they have an unlimited source of the "mystical dust." Before too long, however, the dust settles, and only the container remains, empty and hollow, never to be replenished. They did not understand how to use the mystical dust and, ironically, they have no idea how to replenish their supply. They thought it would last forever. To those who had to endure the showers of power dust, they may have thought it seemed to last forever. But a sprinkling of power dust here and there will last much longer than dumping inappropriate mounds.

Categories of Leadership Power

Power comes to us through a variety of means. Specifically, we can view the acquisition of leadership power in six categories, illustrated in Figure 12.1. Each category is numbered in order of significance in acquiring power for a leadership role. Category 1 is the weakest and most short-lived, whereas Category 6 is the strongest and the most longlasting. However, Categories 1 through 5 are actually part of Category 6. Each one builds on the other and strengthens Category 6. Viewed separately, we can describe each category as such:

Six categories of leadership power.

What you have
1

What you did to earn it
6

Who you know
2

**CATEGORIES OF
LEADERSHIP
POWER**

5
What you have done

3
What you feel

4
What you know

CATEGORY 1: WHAT YOU HAVE

Standing alone, Category 1 is the weakest category for acquiring power for a leadership role. Many people are drawn to materialistic goods, and place people who have a variety of these goods on a pedestal. Some people who are wealthy and have valuable property, spacious homes, or other commodities viewed as "important" use these objects to attract and gain temporary power.

Most people have worked hard all of their lives for their possessions. As a tool for acquiring lasting power over other people, however, it is a weak category. Possessions can be lost or stolen, and if your power base is built only on material objects, your power base is crumbling at you read this.

▲ ▲ ▲

CATEGORY 2: WHO YOU KNOW

You probably have heard the expression, "It's not *what* you know but *who* you know." In today's workplace this often is true. Networking and making contacts are of ultimate importance to most employees today. Nevertheless, a power base built only on "who you know" is weak. Managers, supervisors, and leaders who acquired their position because they "knew the boss" are familiar to us. Many people who acquire power this way rise to the occasion and quickly learn that the boss or the owner can confer position, but not real power. Those who acquire power in this fashion and fail to realize that power is earned through the respect of the people they lead, usually do not succeed in a leadership role. This is not to say that they lose their job or even their role. It is to say, however, that they do not have true power. They may have force, but not responsible power.

ΛDVIҪΣ FꞦΟM Λ MΣNTΟꞦ

Curtis M. Roe,

Training and Recruitment Manager
Las Vegas Hilton,
Las Vegas, NV

Leadership and critical thinking are the most important aspects of my job. So much of my time is spent communicating with employees, managers, and colleagues from other properties. If I fail to consider the short- and long-term consequences of a remark that I make, a concept that I teach, or an action in which I engage, I could lose a student, or worse, I could lose my credibility. What I say in a training class affects the entire workplace. I have to remember that with each statement and each action, I am a leader for my company.

▲ ▲ ▲

CATEGORY 3: WHAT YOU FEEL

What you feel is much more abstract than what you have or who you know.

As I look back on my college education, I realize that higher education gave me the skills to think, to be creative, and to lead. The traditional workplace evolves so quickly with new technology and new concepts that you need to have the basic skills of leadership in order to assist others in their careers. The leadership skills that I learned in college are now imperative to my own success.

Acquiring power by what you feel can be summed up as "leading with a soul." People respect leaders whom they see as reflective and thoughtful. When leaders make decisions with their soul, those who are being led know the difference. This is the beginning of earned power. People begin to respect and appreciate that the leader has taken the time to look at every option, explored many solutions—and taken the human side of matters into consideration. Earning true power begins with soul leadership.

CATEGORY 4: WHAT YOU KNOW

Sometimes older people have difficulty being led by younger people. The younger person feels threatened and sometimes uses too much force, and the older person sees the younger leader as a "hotshot" fresh out of college with no real life experience, just "book knowledge." To a large extent, leadership power is gained through competence and expertise. When the workforce knows that the leader is intelligent, bright, studious, resourceful, and clever, respect and earned power follows. One must be cautioned, however, that real leaders with real power are knowledgeable students, too. They continue to learn from their surroundings. We will return to this topic later in this chapter.

CATEGORY 5: WHAT YOU HAVE DONE

Life experience, properly used, is one of the most powerful tools in leadership and will gain you as much power as any device known. Leaders should be careful, however, not to rely too heavily on the past and, in doing so, overlook current trends and new options. Using what you know is one of the strongest tools for gaining respect and acquiring power. People like working for leaders whom they believe have experience, knowledge, background, and training, They also like working with leaders who know how to use past situations to offer solutions to current problems.

CATEGORY 6: WHAT YOU DID TO EARN IT

Coming full circle, true power is always earned. Power may come from what you have, who you know, what you

ΛDVIÇΣ
CONTINUED.

The one piece of advice that I would offer to you as you begin your career is this: Never be afraid to accept a leadership role in your new job, but, remember, with this role comes immense responsibility to others. Treat others with respect and dignity and those gifts will come back to you.

feel, what you know, and what you have done, but, ultimately, true power is earned. Power can be earned by:

- Respecting other people
- Appreciating the work that people do
- Appreciating what people know
- Demonstrating a genuine interest in colleagues and their families
- Appreciating and calling on others' life experiences
- Being courageous and making fair decisions
- Giving power to others to help themselves (empowering)
- Remaining calm and getting the facts in the face of crisis
- Being a positive, optimistic force
- Using creativity and asking for help
- Providing employees with the tools, support, and training to help them do the best job possible
- Living the motto, "I am a part of a bigger picture."

Powerful leaders enable others to be the very best they can be. They encourage others to explore options and to create new paths. Last, powerful leaders are not challenged or threatened by people who excel.

To Thine Own Self Be True

On the road to leadership, many people forget one of the most important facets of life as a leader. They forget who they are. Worse yet, they never knew. You need to look inside your soul and discover who you really are, where you are going, what you have to offer, where you came from, and what your ultimate potential is.

When was the last time you took a serious look at your life? "I'm too busy" you're probably saying right now. "I have a hectic job . . . I have a family . . . I have to take care of the yard on weekends." Maybe the reason you have so little time on your hands is that you have not taken the time to discover or rediscover your priorities and what is important to your life right now. Many people come up with a new set of goals at the beginning of each year. But how many of us include with that list of goals a listing of what is important in our lives?

The leaders in this world who have the most to offer are those who have spent time with themselves. Leaders who have the greatest impact on humanity have a personal vision. They know what they value, they know their needs, and they understand their abilities.

If we are to truly know ourselves, we must be in tune with many different realms (Pegg, 1994). To be a knowledgeable, caring leader you must care for:

your philosophy	your performance
your purpose	your profits
your people	your prospects
your products	your public responsibility
your public	your planet

This is a daunting task for most people, but remarkable leaders with responsible power know themselves and, in that light, can help others know themselves.

The Human Touch of Leadership

In the world of today, the gap between goals and realization of those goals is wider than at any time in all of history. For never before—in this country and the world over—have the minds of men been so stirred with a ferment of specific wants and desires and demands—and, I might add, of profound fears and hates. It is these wants and demands—and forebodings and hatreds—that have produced a state of excitement, of tension, of revolutionary and often violent turbulence all over the world. This human turbulence is the prime characteristic of these days in which we live. It must be, I think, the main point of reference in assessing the leader's role.

These words could have been written this morning. They were, however, written more than 30 years ago by David Lilienthal (1967). Our times are much the same. At the same time, employees have many different demands. To bring a goal to realization it seems more difficult now than 30 years ago. The workplace is entirely different than it was just 10 years ago. Leaders are faced with issues of paramount importance to employees, such as child care, treatment programs, split workdays, and home offices. How then can leaders provide the best of all possible worlds to this divergent population? How can we, in a world of vast and expanding technology, touch the lives of our employees?

We can begin by realizing that technology and gadgetry are not panaceas for productivity, profit, or relationships. Leaders must explore the nontraditional side of establishing work relationships in this age of little or no contact. A study done by the Public Agenda Foundation found that the number-one quality people want in a job today is "to work with people who treat me with respect." Other desired qualities were leaders who listen, leaders who encourage employees to think, and leaders who provide information. These are some of the qualities that effective leaders should use to create a more "human" leadership style. Other ways of putting the human touch back into leadership are:

- Creating a communication plan that incorporates all employees and customers
- Asking questions of your employees and customers
- Getting to know your employees on a first-name basis
- Finding out what your employees need and want in their jobs
- Having frequent (but needed) meetings to discuss issues and plans
- Spending time "on the floor" with your employees

Wayne Calloway, PepsiCo's CEO, explains human touch in this fashion:

> The point is people. Making sure they are learning. Making sure they are happy. Making sure they are proud. Those ends, he asserts, create PepsiCo's most powerful competitive edge. (Farkas and DeBacker, 1996)

Perhaps the motto "The Point is People" sums up what human touch is all about.

The 10 Basic Qualities of Remarkable Leadership

Literally thousands of lists have been generated suggesting what leaders should possess to be successful. We have taken what we believe to be the best of these lists and compiled the results into the 10 basic qualities of remarkable leadership.

1. Vision
2. Knowledgeable students
3. Courage
4. Motivational skills
5. Fairness and equity
6. Team building skills
7. Change agents
8. Communication skills

9. Conflict managers

10. Accept responsibility

VISION

A vision portrays how the future is supposed to look. It provides people with a framework to help them understand. A leader's vision gives direction and asks: *Where* should we be? *When* should we be there? *Why* should we be there? *Where* will we concentrate our resources? *How* will our lives be changed?

KNOWLEDGEABLE STUDENTS

Remarkable leaders are students of the world. They learn from their surroundings and the people with whom they work. They are unafraid to admit they do not know something and unafraid to seek the answers.

COURAGE

Remarkable leaders accept the challenges of leadership and the trials and strains it brings. They are fearless in the face of adversity, change, apathy, and frustration.

MOTIVATIONAL SKILLS

Remarkable leaders have the skills to motivate the masses. Remarkable leaders also know that not every employee will be motivated. As leaders, they recognize that there always will be people in the workplace who are bitter, negative, and hateful. Not all employees will react with enthusiasm.

FAIRNESS AND EQUITY

Leaders treat each employee with respect. Leaders also treat employees with fairness and equity.

TEAM BUILDING SKILLS

Henry Ford once said, "Coming together is a beginning; staying together is progress; working together is success." Remarkable leaders are able to do all three. They can bring people together, help them stay together, and, most important, help them work together toward a common goal.

CHANGE AGENTS

No change is easy. Even good change is sometimes stressful and hard. The leader is responsible for easing the transition and making the change as stress-free as possible.

COMMUNICATION SKILLS

Opening the lines of communication—verbal, nonverbal, written, and technological—can save more time, money, hard feelings, and frustration than any other skill.

CONFLICT MANAGERS

Leaders deal with conflict quickly and seriously. To ignore conflict is to increase its power over the organization or team. In Chapter 11 we explored conflict management in more detail.

ACCEPT RESPONSIBILITY

Remarkable leaders accept total responsibility for their actions. They do not try to pass blame. They do not lie to avoid reprimand. They do not say, "but I was . . .," "if only you had . . .," or "I was going to . . . ." They accept responsibility for their actions, the actions of their employees, and ultimately the actions of their organization.

12 Results of Remarkable Leadership

The entire concept of leadership is to assist employees and the company in reaching goals and making life and work more pleasant. The benefits of remarkable leadership include:

harmony	ethical decisions
candor	individuality
openness	productivity
trust	two-way open communication
understanding	participation
challenging situations	assessment and feedback

References

Farkas, C., and DeBacker, P. (1996). *Maximum Leadership: The World's Leading CEO's Share Their Five Strategies for Success*. New York: Henry Holt and Company.

Lilienthal, D. (1967). *Management: A Humanist Art*. New York: Columbia University Press.

McLean, J., and Weitzel, W. (1992). *Leadership—Magic, Myth or Method?* New York: American Management Association.

Pegg, Mike. (1994). *Positive Leadership: How to Build a Winning Team*. San Diego: Pheiffer and Co.

CAPSTONES

FOR LEADERSHIP

Leadership is all about
human beings.

▲

We should strive to be a leader
of people, not a manager of things.

▲

Power is different from force.

▲

Power based on what you have and who you know is
not as "real" as power that is earned.

▲

In becoming a leader, you will have to maintain your own value
system and be true to yourself.

UNIT THREE

Life and Personal Enrichment

ADVICE FROM A PEER

Dana Bennett,
Graduate: Physical Therapy
Medical College of Georgia

Webster's Dictionary defines potential as "capable of doing or being: inherent capability of doing anything." The key parts of this definition are the verbs "being" and "doing." As a recent college graduate, I am thankful that someone took the time to help me understand that one's potential is a great as one's dreams. As you graduate from college and enter the world of work, it is important to know that you, too, have the ability to do anything that you can dream. Never let anyone put boundaries on you, your future, or your potential.

Below I have laid out a plan for success using the word *potential*. This plan has helped me achieve many of my dreams, and I refer to it as I move forward in developing my own potential.

P Prioritize: Put your priorities in order, remembering what makes you happy.

O Opportunity: Opportunity rarely knocks twice, so answer each one carefully.

T Treat: Treat others with respect, and this will come back to you.

E Exercise: Exercise your mind, body, and soul on a daily basis.

N Never: Never lose sight of what really matters to you.

T Timeliness: Keep up with recent facts, technology, and trends. Stay on top.

I Initiative: Take charge, set your goals high, and polish the leader in you.

A Acknowledge: Always pay homage to those who helped you along the way.

L Leave: Leave work at work and home at home.

Managing Your Post-College Finances

I've been rich and I've been poor—rich is better.

SOPHIE TUCKER

Most college students can't wait to get a "real" job and buy all the things they could not afford as a student. If you earn the typical starting salary and are totally on your own, you probably will find that you still can't buy everything you would like to purchase. Before you rush out and buy a new car and a new wardrobe, give yourself time to understand your total financial picture to avoid making some big mistakes. You've waited this long. Be patient a little longer. If you never have had to manage a budget, financial management may be more difficult than you imagined. You must keep in mind that you have to be able to pay bills!

While preparing to graduate from college and immediately after you graduate, you will be faced with many decisions. If you have not done so already, you will have to make a decision about which job to accept, what area to live in, what kind of home you can afford, whether you should keep a car you own now or purchase a new one, whether to get married now or in the near future, whether to have a roommate or to live alone—the list goes on and on.

Most college graduates deal with this list of decisions, and most make reasonable decisions. This list, however, does not include one of the most important priorities: financial management. Most people fail to give the same kind of attention to financial matters that they do to other major areas of their lives. The average person spends more time deciding which programs to watch on TV than on which financial choices to make. Young college graduates often assume that they do not have enough money to manage and these decisions will be important only when they are much older. *The first day you go to work is the day you should start planning for retirement and financial security!*

Some of the decisions mentioned earlier will have a major impact on your life and your lifestyle, but none will be more important than making wise financial-management decisions. These decisions include daily budgeting, credit-card choices, retirement options, savings programs, and benefit packages. Making the right financial decisions requires taking time to educate yourself about the options. You cannot afford *not* to prepare yourself to make wise financial decisions!

To help you better determine your financial picture and plan for the future, this chapter will discuss the following topics:

▲ Studying finance

▲ Financial terminology

stocks	IRA	compound interest
mutual funds	SEP-IRA	discretionary income
401-K	money market	profit sharing

▲ Tax deferment and tax sheltering

▲ Creating a budget

▲ Avoiding the worst kind of debt—credit cards

▲ Repaying student loans

Learning About Financial Management

A first step in financial management is to decide to become knowledgeable about finances. If you are taking this course as a first-semester senior and still have an elective, one of the best things you can do for yourself is to take a personal-finance course. If you can't take a course now, you can educate yourself in other ways. When you graduate, you should continue your financial education by enrolling in financial-management seminars and by reading financial publications such as *Fortune, Forbes, Money, Successful Investing,* and others. The more you read, the more likely you will be to become a successful financial manager and investor.

Although it is fine to listen to your friends' advice and the counsel of financial managers, including stock brokers, you need to be able to make your own decisions and to plan your own investment strategy. You may overhear a "hot tip" in the elevator at work, but chances are slim that acting on this tip will be a wise decision. Successful investing requires a plan and the discipline to stick to it.

You will work hard to earn your salary, and you can let it slip away from you on frivolous items and poor decisions, or you can decide to manage your money and become financially secure. If you make up your mind to retire comfortably, even to be wealthy, you can do so by reading and learning, making wise decisions, and disciplining yourself to save and invest on a regular and continuing basis.

Discipline is extremely important to your financial success because it is much easier to spend than to save and much more rewarding to purchase clothes, jewelry, cars, and trips now than to struggle to save 10 percent of your income. If you can focus on this fact, however, it might help you to save: If you can save now and invest wisely, the time will come when you can have almost anything you want! You can retire early and travel; you can educate your children; you can live in a nice home and drive luxury cars; you can spend money without worrying about every dime. Delayed gratification is the first key. Starting early is the second.

You also will want to read financial books that set forth strategies for accumulating wealth and planning for retirement. Several are listed at the end of this chapter as references.

Financial Terms You Need to Know

Perhaps you selected a major in college that had nothing to do with finance and you don't know where to start. Although we cannot provide in this chapter all the information you need to know, we will cover many important financial terms and concepts.

One rule you need to remember about investing is: If it sounds too good to be true, it probably is. Do not lose your hard-earned money to some unscrupulous person who will squander your money on some foolhardy scheme. Select your investments with great care. Your future depends on it!

Some definitions of terms you need to know are provided below.

Stock
:   A share of a company. The more shares you own, the more your investment is valued. The value of stocks can go up and down. The best strategy is usually to choose highly respected companies, invest on a continuous basis, and avoid buying and selling frequently. Every time you buy or sell, you must pay a fee. These fees eat into your profits. Although some people have been highly successful as day traders, most people do not have the time or the knowledge to engage in this practice.

Mutual fund
:   A pool of stocks managed by a professional. You invest in a mutual fund by buying shares. These shares entitle you to a portion of the fund's earnings, depending on how many shares you have. Many people prefer to invest in this manner because they don't have to select the stocks, nor do they have to make decisions about when to buy and sell. The professional manager makes these decisions. In the beginning, this is probably the best choice for inexperienced investors.

    More than 2,800 funds are available from which to choose, making it difficult to decide what to select. You may want to seek professional help in the beginning. If you do decide to enlist the help of a financial planner, you need to seek references, check credentials, and invest a small amount in the beginning until you trust this person's judgment.

401-K	A tax-deferred plan that enables you to save while putting off paying taxes on your earnings. Your company may use this type of program to allow you to save.
IRA	An individual retirement account. This plan allows certain people to invest up to $2,000 a year in a tax-sheltered program depending on one's income. "Tax-sheltered" means you don't pay taxes on the money until you withdraw it, usually at retirement.
SEP-IRA	A tax-deferred plan designed for self-employed people. You may do extra work such as writing, consulting, or computer work in addition to your regular job, perhaps using a home office. In some cases you can contribute to a SEP-IRA, which gives you an additional way to invest for the future. SEP-IRAs allow you to invest in the same types of investments as other funds.
Money market	A type of investment that pays interest based on the current prime rate.
Compound interest	A method of figuring interest that allows you to collect interest on your investment. This interest is added back to your investment, enabling you to collect interest on interest. This principle is what makes it possible to earn large amounts of money on investments over a number of years.
Discretionary income	Income that you can choose how to spend; it does not have to be spent on recurring budget items.
Profit-sharing	A program that many companies offer to their employees, enabling them to share in the profits by investing in the company. If your company has such a plan, you should take advantage of it, although it usually is not required. As a rule, you must be with a company for a specified length of time before you are eligible for profit-sharing. Increasingly, companies are using profit-sharing as a retirement program—meaning that you will have no other company-contributed funds when you retire. If this is the case with your company, profit-sharing is immensely important to you.

Profit-sharing programs deduct a portion of your earnings—up to 20 percent in some companies. This money is deducted *before* you pay taxes, so it is *tax-deferred*, or *tax-sheltered*, meaning you save this money before you pay taxes. You don't pay taxes until you withdraw the money, either at retirement or at some other time. If you withdraw any portion of this tax-deferred fund, you are assessed a penalty, plus you will have to pay ordinary income taxes when your taxes come due that year. Unless you have a dire emergency, you should not withdraw your retirement funds because, typically, they are never replaced.

Some programs allow you to borrow against your retirement fund, usually at a lower rate of interest than you would receive from a bank. This money, however, must be paid back within a specified time or you will be penalized and you will be required to pay taxes on it that year. Usually it is best not to borrow from this fund because, while the loan is outstanding, your fund is not earning money on that amount. One of the secrets to investing is long-term compound interest.

Most companies have a *matching component*. Based on the company's profitability, they will give you money in addition to what you have in your account.

Companies have different plans. One plan works like this: The company will match the first 5 percent you contribute, dollar for dollar, and the next 5 percent at 50 cents on the dollar.

For example, if you earn $30,000 and you elect to invest 10 percent of your salary in

ΛDVIÇΣ FROM Λ MΣNTOR

Timothy S. Rice,

Financial Advisor,

Waddell & Reed, Inc.,

Shawnee Mission, KS

Some of the earliest lessons I learned from my parents and grandparents were how to manage money. I thank them every day for those valuable life lessons. Because of their care and respect for financial management, I was able to learn how to save and invest money and, most importantly, how to avoid credit-card and loan debt.

Today, as a Financial Advisor, I handle millions of dollars for clients, friends, and family. If there is one piece of advice that I offer them all, it is this: "Never underestimate the power of compound interest!" I would offer you the same advice as you start out in the world of work. Even if you save and invest only ten or twenty dollars per week, you'll be amazed at how that money grows and how delightful it is to have money for your first down payment on a home, money for your child's college fund, or savings for your early retirement.

profit-sharing, the company would deduct $3,000 a year from your pre-tax income, meaning you would be taxed on only $27,000 at this time. Assume your company matches the first 50 percent of your contribution. This will add another $1,500 to your contribution. Now assume that the company matches the next 50 percent of your contribution at 50 cents for each dollar you contribute. This adds still another $750 to your fund. At the end of only one year, you will have accumulated $5,250. If you continue to do this year after year—invest wisely and do not withdraw your money—you will accumulate a sizeable amount of money.

Companies normally have several options for investing your money, including company stock. Although you should invest some of your funds in company stock, you should diversify and channel a portion of your contributions into other options, such as stocks other than your company's and mutual funds.

As a rule, if you leave a company, you will be allowed to take with you only the portion of the contributions you have made to your retirement fund unless you are *vested*. Vested means that you have worked for the company a certain number of years, usually 5. If you are vested and you leave the company, you will be allowed to take your entire retirement fund with you. Naturally, if you have worked for a company 4 years and receive a good offer from another company, a major decision is whether to take the job or to remain with the current company and become vested. This would depend on how much money your company has contributed to your fund and how much increase in salary the new company is offering. The important thing is to decide based on knowledge and not on a whim that could cost you greatly over the long term.

If you leave a company and have a sum of money to take with you, you must not spend this money. Many people make this mistake. With the money, they buy a car or a boat or furniture or clothes or take a trip—and the money is gone forever on depreciable items; $10,000 spent on a boat will be worth nothing 30 years from now. The same $10,000 invested at 10 percent and compounded annually, will be *worth $174,494 30 years later*. If you invest $10,000 at 10 percent and the interest is compounded monthly, it will be worth $198,373 at the end of 30 years. Again, delayed gratification is crucial.

Another reason not to spend this money is income taxes. If you re-invest these funds within 60 days, the taxes will continue to be deferred. If, how-

ΛDVIÇΣ
CONTINUED.

Some people tell me, "I don't want to save; I want to live now!" I understand their point. However, with proper financial planning, you can do both. Pay yourself first! Starting with your first paycheck, put away 10 percent and treat this money as if it was going toward a debt—"The Bank of Me!"

ever, you do not reinvest this money, you will owe ordinary income taxes on the entire amount. For example, if you are in a 28 percent tax bracket and your fund amounts to $10,000, you will owe $2,800 in additional income taxes that year. If, on the other hand, you place this money in a tax-deferred fund, the $2,800 that would have gone to taxes is protected and continues to earn interest for your retirement. Depending on whether the interest is compounded monthly or annually, $2,800 over a period of 30 years invested at an annual rate of 8 percent will amount to $28,175 yearly or $30,620 monthly. Clearly, it pays in the long run to resist the urge to splurge and spend money that should be invested and protected.

Another term you may hear is "rolling over" funds. This means moving money from one company's retirement fund to another company's retirement fund.

Budgeting: Making Wise Use of Your Money

Most people do not budget. They have a reasonable idea of what they can spend and how much they require to cover the house payment, car payment, food, utilities, and the like, but it is just a guess. They have never sat down and decided to live within their income and to use their money wisely. As a result, they are often strapped for money, late with payments, and have little or no savings.

Many people do not use their discretionary income wisely. This is the difference in being secure and being broke. The information in this chapter is intended to help you choose how you spend your money and to instill in you the belief that money management is an everyday process. If you are going to be financially secure, you cannot afford to live day-to-day and hand-to-mouth with no plan for accumulating wealth.

As a new college graduate, you will be wise to establish a budget and live within your means. Some of your expenses will vary, depending on whether you have a roommate or a spouse or whether you live alone. In this scenario, we will assume that you live alone, that you make $30,000 a year, and that you are contributing 10 percent to your company's tax-deferred profit-sharing program so you will be taxed on only $27,000. Let's also assume that you have company benefits that provide you full coverage for your personal health insurance and 1-1/2 times your salary in life insurance so you don't have to spend any of your salary on those items.

For purposes of this exercise, let's assume that you are in the 28 percent federal income tax bracket and that you live in a state that has a 7 percent state income tax. In addition, FICA taxes (Social Security and Medicare) will be deducted before you receive your take-home pay. These will amount to 7.65 percent of your salary.

When you deduct your federal taxes of $7,560 plus your state income taxes of $1,890 plus your FICA taxes of $2,065, your annual take-home pay is now $15,485, assuming you have no more deductions taken from your salary. Dividing this amount by 12 months, you have $1,290 a month to budget.

Because costs vary greatly from one part of the country to another, estimating expenses is difficult, but for purposes of this exercise, assume the following monthly expenses:

Rent—$500

Car payment—$250

Car insurance (this varies widely from state-to-state, especially if you have traffic violations)—$50

Gas—$80

Utilities (heat, electricity, water)—$80

You have only about $330 left for food, clothes, entertainment, telephone, cable TV, and so on. Right away it becomes apparent that having someone with whom to share expenses might be an advantage. Complete the other items of this budget with amounts that you would allocate if this were your personal situation.

Food—

Entertainment—

Telephone—

Clothes—

Credit cards—

Student loans (if applicable)—

Miscellaneous (shampoo, deodorant, magazines, etc.)—

Savings (you probably think you won't have any need for this, but you really do need to have money in a savings account for emergencies; financial experts use a figure of 3 months salary)—

This exercise is usually painful for college students but is a valuable lesson to learn as early as possible. The good news is that you can increase your income and lessen the pressure on your budget, provided you realize that no matter how much money you make, it is easy to spend it unwisely on frivolous items that are soon forgotten.

Though you are urged to make wise financial decisions, you are encouraged to enjoy life and not be so thrifty that you don't allow yourself to spend money on things and items that bring you pleasure and enjoyment. As you learned in Chapter 4, professional appearance is important. Looking your best requires that you spend money on clothes. You can be a wise consumer and still dress nicely by shopping for sales.

The Worst Kind of Debt: Credit Cards

The time to begin thinking about financial management is now. Actually, you may have made some decisions already that you need to rethink immediately. For example, if you got the "credit-card-itis" disease in college, you must do something *now* if you are ever going to be financially secure.

Most college students receive several credit cards as soon as they graduate from high school. By the time they graduate, many have accumulated sizeable debts. Some college students have several credit cards on which they have charged the limit. Thinking that they will pay off their credit cards when they get a full-time job, these students have been making the minimum payment most of the time. They now have two problems: a sizeable debt with a high interest rate, and if they have been late with payments, a poor credit record.

Making late payments only two or three times can reflect poorly on your credit rating. A poor credit record can keep you from being able to buy a house or a car or get a loan. *Credit-card debt is the worst kind of debt you can have!* If you have credit-card debt, the first move you need to make is to pay off these debts.

To understand how important getting rid of this kind of debt is, consider this: If you have a debt of $1,000 and make only minimum payments, it will take more than 15 years to pay off this debt at a cost of more than $2,000 in interest.

So what should you do if you are one of these students who has accumulated credit-card debts? First, cut up all your credit cards except one that requires you to pay the balance every month. Make a decision not to use this card unless you absolutely have to until you have paid off your credit-card debts.

Credit-card companies usually charge exorbitant rates from 18 percent to 21 percent. This means that if you are making the minimum payment every month on a sizeable credit card debt and don't even add new charges, it will take years to pay off this debt. Obviously, this isn't the way to go. There has to be another solution.

If you already have a job and your company has a credit union, you can try to borrow the money at a much lower rate of interest to cover all your credit-card debts. Instead of making several small payments at 21 percent interest, you can consolidate your debts and make one large payment at an interest rate about half the one you are paying on credit cards.

Another source may be a bank where you have had a checking account. You may not want your parents to know about all the money you owe, but if all else fails, they might go with you to a bank and co-sign a note with you to help you borrow the money. Facing the wrath of upset parents is not as bad as trying to manage out-of-control debt on a beginning salary. You will probably just dig the hole deeper unless you can make a plan for getting this monkey off your back. When you borrow the money, establish a payment that you know you can make comfortably. In time, you will get this debt paid and earn back your good credit rating.

When you get out of credit-card debt, promise yourself that this will *never* happen to you again. If you are fortunate and have not committed this financial mistake, learn from others' mistakes. *Never* charge things you can't afford to pay for at the end of the month. You cannot be financially successful until you have mastered this rule! One more time— cut up all your credit cards except one that requires you to pay it off each month and preferably awards you frequent-flyer miles for every dollar you charge. One of the rewa for fiscal responsibility can be a free trip to a place you always wanted to visit.

A great deal goes into wise management of money and investments. This chapter merely scratches the surface of what there is to know. Still, it should instill in you the importance of wise financial decisions to your future.

Repaying Student Loans

If you are one of the many students who has borrowed money to go to college, you may be concerned about your ability to repay the loans. Before you leave your college campus, find out everything you need to know about your loan, and determine your options. Some of the most pertinent points about student loans are as follows.

- You have a legal obligation to repay your student loans with interest.
- You should get the addresses and phone numbers of lenders before you leave college.

- Certain circumstances, such as graduate school, allow you to defer your payments. A deferment allows you to postpone your payments.
- Learn all the options you have for repaying your loans. Based on your salary, expenses, and budget, decide which one is best for you.
- If for some reason you cannot make your payment, let the lender know immediately. This is not something that will go away. You do not want to default on your loan, as this will cause you to have a bad credit rating.

References

Abentrod, Susan. (1996). *10 Minute Guide to Beating Debt*. Alpha Books.

Hetzer, Barbara. (1997). *10 Minute Guide to Working With a Financial Advisor*. Alpha Books.

Orman, Suze. (1997). *The 9 Steps of Financial Freedom*. Springfield, MA: Crown Publishers.

Rye, David. (1999). *1001 Ways to Save, Grow, and Invest Your Money*. Santa Barbara, CA: Career Press.

Stanley, Thomas J., and Danko, William D. (1998). *The Millionaire Next Door: The Surprising Secrets of America's Wealthy*. New York: Pocket Books.

Tyson, Eric. (1997). *Personal Finance for Dummies* (2d ed.). New York: IDG Books Worldwide.

CAPSTONES

FOR FINANCIAL SECURITY

Delayed gratification will reap rewards in the long run.

▲

Credit-card debt is to be avoided at all costs.

▲

Making financial decisions requires strong self-discipline.

▲

The power of compound interest and reinvested earnings is substantial.

▲

Before graduating, students should learn all they can about personal financial management.

▲

Students should develop a financial plan that includes short-term and long-range goals.

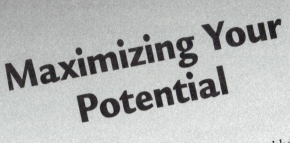

Maximizing Your Potential

Happiness comes only when we push our brains and hearts to the farthest reaches of which we are capable. The purpose of life is to matter—to count, to stand for something, to have it make some difference that we lived at all.

LEO BUSCAGLIA

In the ancient religion of Hinduism, the second oldest religion in the world, with 330 million gods, lies the Sanskrit secret doctrine, the *Upanishads*. From this doctrine come the words: "You are what your deep, driving desire is. As your desire is, so is your will. As your will is, so is your deed. As your deed is, so is your destiny." Perhaps one of the most important questions in this book, and certainly in this chapter, is this: What is your destiny?

In truth, few people spend time thinking about that question, and fewer still make the effort to live and work *toward* their destiny. Further, some people believe, and some religions teach, that our destiny is predetermined. Whether you have spent time thinking about your destiny, working toward your destiny, or believing that your destiny is not within your control, you can take actions to understand your place in the world more clearly. Each person can examine his or her life, set goals, explore his or her value system, integrity and ethics, and question the reasons for being here.

In an effort to understand more about your personal life, your values, goals, potential, and direction in life, this chapter will discuss the following topics:

▲ The end of your life

▲ A definition of success

▲ Self-analysis

▲ Exploring what you want to be

▲ The pursuit of joy

    work

    family/friends

    leisure time

    growth and discovery

    giving

The End of Your Life: The Obituary

The end of your life—not a pleasant thought, is it? You are graduating from college, and we are talking about your death. There is method to our madness, however. If you have ever read an obituary in the newspaper, you know the typical content: date of birth, age, family members, career, religious affiliation, community involvement, and achievements. If you think about it, an obituary is really nothing more than a brief synopsis of a person's life. "So," you say, "What does this have to do with my life? I'm not dead yet." True. But one day you will be, and the overriding question is this: What will you want your obituary to say? How will the words and pages of your life read?

Before you read any farther, pretend for a moment that you have lived to reach the age of 90 years. Treat your obituary as a goal statement, and jot down some of the things you would like to have people read about you at the end of your life.

That was hard, and maybe a little sad, wasn't it? The end of your life is not pleasant to think about, regardless of your current age. The reason we ask you to do this exercise is that, like any goal, if you don't know what you are striving toward, how will you ever get there? If you don't know what you want the end of your life to look like, how will you ever achieve the words and statements you would like to have said or written about you at the end of it? This is the purpose of beginning with the end in mind.

As we move through this chapter, you will have the opportunity to reflect on many aspects of your life, including:

- your chosen profession
- your value system
- your family and friends
- your leisure time
- how you define success

Success On Your Terms

Are you a success? If the answer that first comes to your mind is "yes," on what terms do you base your answer? Do you feel successful because you are about to graduate from college? Do you feel successful because you have money? Or do you feel successful because you have an abundance of friends? If the answer is "no," why do you think you are not a success? Is it lack of money, the wrong career or job, no close friends, poor grades? It is important to know why we feel that we are or are not a success.

The great American educator, and founder of the Tuskegee Institute in Alabama, George Washington Carver, once said, "I have learned that success is to be measured not so much by the position one has reached in life as by the obstacles which he has overcome trying to succeed." What is your definition of success? Arkoff (1995) suggests that we might grade the success of our lives on the same scale as we are graded in college: A, B, C, D, F. "If your life were to end today," he asks, "what grade could be inscribed on your headstone or be written in red on your box of ashes?"

Why is it important to even think of grading our lives or writing our obituary? It is important because both cause us to pause and reflect on the quality of our life. Both cause us to examine our actions, our goals, and our worth. Years ago a physician interviewed people who had been clinically dead, but survived. The doctor asked them to think about and determine the value of their lives. "One of the most important lessons they brought back from this close encounter with death was the need to love others more acceptingly, more deeply and more profoundly" (Moody, 1975, in Arkoff, 1995).

Some people relate success to money, love, power, prestige, or influence. Some relate success to their degree of happiness. Myers (1992) found through surveys that the following things facilitate happiness:

- Supportive friendships
- A socially intimate, sexually warm, equitable marriage
- Faith
- Challenging work
- Positive self-esteem
- Realistic goals
- A fit and healthy body

You, and only you, can determine what the word success means to you. Your parents, friends, professors, or rivals cannot answer this for you. They may have influence, but you and your heart will determine the answer.

Who Are You Now?

The questions keep coming, don't they? Is it important to know who you are at this moment? Is it important to ever know the answer? Most psychologists would suggest that it *is* important. It is important to know who you are because this is another road to finding your true self. Most people answer the question, "who are you?" with statements such as: I'm a student; I'm a mother or father; I'm a son or daughter; I'm a future nurse, lawyer, teacher, or engineer. These answers are fine, but they don't answer the question. They answer *what* you are, not *who* you are.

Without knowing *who* you are, you will have a difficult time developing a positive outlook or a positive self-image. Who and how you perceive yourself affects the way you move and live in this world. It affects the way you treat others. Take, for example, the person who walks into a grocery store or school with an arsenal of weapons and opens fire. One of the reasons this person has no value for your life, or the life of your friends and family, is that he or she does not value or understand his or her *own* life.

As you begin to investigate and understand more about your life and who you are, you may find that you are more than one person. No, we're not talking about the multiple personalities of Sybil or the different faces of Eve, but you may find that your personality changes with the environment or different situations.

The ancient philosopher Socrates said, "The unexamined life is not worth living." You can begin to examine your life and study the question, "Who are you?" in several ways.

- Spend time each day with yourself, alone, in a quiet place, and think about your day, your actions, your growth, and your treatment of others
- What are your true loves?
- What do you honestly value and why?
- If money were not a problem or did not enter the equation, what would you do for the rest of your life? Why are you not doing it?
- Do you rationalize your behaviors so that you don't have to deal with them?
- Do you deny things in your life that are unpleasant or less than favorable?
- Do you stray away from people who have personality traits that you do not like in yourself?
- What are your standards for yourself?
- How do you handle failure, setbacks, and adversity?

Noted psychologist and therapist Carl Rogers (1961) quotes Kierkegaard, a Danish religious philosopher, as saying, "Each of us struggles to be that self which one truly is." As you continue your quest to answer, "Who are you," you might consider the following words by Bessie Delany (1994). "I'd say one of the most important things is the ability to create joy in your life. Of course, at my age, it's a joy to be breathing." She was 103 years of age when she wrote these words.

What Do You Value?

Let's pretend for a moment that you are going to a strange auction. At this auction, you can't purchase any material items such as antique rugs or sterling silver. You can purchase only personal qualities. If you attend such an auction and have only $1,000 to spend on any of the items listed below, how would you spend the money? You could bid all $1,000 on one item, or you could bid $500 on two items, or $100 on 10 items. How would you spend your money on the following?

- A great personality
- Wonderful friends
- A meaningful religious faith
- A marriage or partnership that is full of love
- A successful career
- A life of security
- A life of control and power
- Ultimate wisdom
- Unlimited pleasure
- Revenge against an enemy or rival
- The answer to the question, "What is the meaning of life?"
- Successful children
- The ability to solve one of society's ills
- A peaceful soul
- Health
- The ability not to age
- A life lived to its full potential
- Effective communication skills
- The love of your parents
- Days filled with leisure time

Your behavior and actions at this "auction" will tell you much about what you value and what you hold dear.

When we examine values, we begin to understand that many variables enter the picture. Values differ because of age, gender, sexual orientation, culture, marital status, parental status, religion, and material wealth, to name a few. Not even life holds the same value for all people.

The kamikaze pilots in World War II valued and honored their duty to their country more than they valued life. So, how do we know if what we value is "good?" Abe Arkoff (1995) suggests five criteria by which we can judge our own value system: explicitness, consistency, flexibility, realism, and satisfaction.

1. *Explicitness* asks how well we understand our own values. Arkoff suggests that when we run across someone who does not value the same things we value, we begin to understand how much we value that "thing." As an example: If you truly value education but have a roommate who does not and is academically dismissed, you began to understand what an education means to you. You begin to value education more.

2. *Consistency* implies how loyal we are to our value system. If you value your health but go bungee jumping, you may be at a crossroad with your value system. If you were taught that gay people are immoral and indecent but your best friend in college is gay and you find those stereotypes to be untrue, you would have to seriously evaluate your value system. As we grow older and move beyond what we previously learned from our parents, neighbors, friends, and religion, we may have to adjust our value system to be consistent with our new knowledge and understanding.

3. *Flexibility* means bending your value system a bit and forming some compromises. A compromising value system may seem contradictory, but the raw truth is that life happens! Change happens! Compromise happens! Consider the case of the co-worker who slacks off and does little for the company. You are placed on a team with him, and your performance rating is contingent on how well the team performs a task. You happen to value hard work and deplore slackers. You value independence, and you value others who pull their weight. In this instance, however, your value system may have to be more flexible than usual, and you may have to help, prod and coach your team member so the entire team looks good in the end.

4. *Realism* is knowing what is possible versus what is not possible. This criterion deals with knowing how to set your values and actions so they are attainable. An example is a person who has, over the years, built up in his or her mind an image of the perfect person with whom to marry or form a partnership. This ideal—perfect, beautiful, giving, devoted—does not exist. Realism in values does not ask you to "settle," but realism does suggest that you understand that no person or mate is perfect.

5. *Satisfaction* is the sense of fulfillment in life. Ask yourself this question: "Does my value system bring me satisfaction?" If you value money, are you satisfied with only money? Would you be happier if you were to have money

and close friends and a caring mate? If you value materialistic goods such as a fine home with expensive furnishings, does this satisfy you? You've worked for years to complete your degree so you can find a satisfying career. You will be the judge as to whether your first job out of college is satisfying. If you find that your job or even your career choice is not satisfying, you will have some hard decisions to make.

ADVICE FROM A MENTOR

Dr. Martin L. Schwartz,

Veterinarian
Park La Brea Veterinarian Care,
Los Angeles, CA

I have been a veterinarian for over 15 years. In that time, I have never once dreaded going to work in the morning. This is because I see every day as a new adventure. I love my job and don't think of it as work. I think of it as something that keeps my mind occupied: an occupation, not a job.

It is unusual for a graduate's first job to be the one that becomes a lifelong career. Unfortunately, life is not that simple. Usually you will find a company that suits you at first and you work there a while, and then you move on for whatever reason. But, if you are wise, whether you like your colleagues or not, you will open your mind and your eyes and learn every lesson possible from them.

That is the first piece of advice that I would offer as you begin your career: Learn something from your colleagues and peers every day! Learn from their mistakes and shortcomings, and from their successes and positive points. Use the time in your early jobs to learn, to grow, and to develop a vision. Save these lessons; write them

The Pursuit of Joy

Motivation is a strange thing. It seems infectious to some and contagious to others. Sometimes it comes with great force and other times it seems elusive. Why do some people seem to be more motivated than others to find joy? We have all been motivated by something at one point or another, but why? What causes us to have that driving force to succeed, to be more, to find joy, to be happy, to get that college degree, or to succeed in one's first job? Two possible reasons are intrinsic motivation and extrinsic motivation.

Motivation that stems from factors such as interest or curiosity is called intrinsic motivation. When we are intrinsically motivated, we do not need incentives or punishments, because the activity itself is rewarding. In contrast, when we do something in order to earn a grade or reward, avoid punishment, please the teacher, or for some other reason that has very little to do with the task itself, we experience extrinsic motivation. (Woolfolk, 1998)

The pursuit of joy is intrinsic. We pursue joy and happiness not for a reward but, instead, for the act itself. Joy comes in as many different forms as the people who pursue it. Some find joy in work. Others find it in leisure activities, family, personal growth, or giving. We will examine some of the activities that bring joy.

▲ ▲ ▲

JOY IN SELF-GROWTH AND DISCOVERY

Some people find joy in learning more about themselves and their purpose in life, developing a vision, exploring their potential, strengthening their soul, or solidifying their life's philosophy. Deepak Chopra (1994) suggests that one way to begin a journey in self-growth and discovery is to practice silence: "There is a prayer in *A Course in Miracles* that states, 'Today, I shall judge nothing that occurs.' Non-judgement creates silence in your mind." He believes that, through this silence, we can begin to access our own potential.

ΛDVIϹΣ CONTINUED. down and file them away so that later, you will be able to draw from your experiences with that company and the people there.

The second piece of advice that I would offer is to fight the dragon of becoming jaded. There is no worse thing than thinking that you know it all, for when you start believing that you do know it all, you stop learning and growing. In my profession we call this "continuing education." I go to symposia, which feature lectures from the most prominent professors from the most prestigious universities in the nation, and this keeps my mind open to change. I've learned that you never know it all. A great part of this lesson in my profession is listening to my clients' description of their pets' illnesses. If I fail to listen, I fail!

These two pieces of advice helped me beyond measure as I opened my own veterinary hospital. Learning from others and keeping my ears open help me maintain interest in my profession. If you lose interest in, and passion for, your profession, it becomes drudgery, and then you get up in the morning dreading your career.

William James, an American psychologist, postulated that humans use only 10 percent of their brain's capacity and thus never really understanding or using much of their potential. Otto (1972) found that if we were to use only half of our brain, we could learn 40 languages with little difficulty. Many psychologists, sociologists, therapists, philosophers, medical personnel, and religious figures agree that we do not know the limits of human potential.

So what are some of the factors that you must overcome to begin using more of your potential? At the forefront is fear—fear of failure, fear of rejection, fear of growth, fear of truth. Other factors include prejudice, lack of role models and mentors, a low self-image, comparing ourselves to others who have done more, a need for security, learned helplessness, and—to be honest—laziness.

To begin to discover more about your potential and grow as a human being, you might consider the following:

- Work to overcome your fears
- Take positive risks every day
- Enlist friends and family to help you
- Stop comparing yourself to others
- Surround yourself with people whom you admire and consider to be using their potential
- Take on projects that are hard and maybe even out of your league so that you can expand your knowledge
- Learn to question assumptions
- Strive to remove biases and prejudices from your life
- Continue your education through graduate school, seminars, and lectures
- Don't be afraid of change and growth; embrace it
- Join organizations that promote growth and self-expansion
- Read, and put into practice, self-help advice from books and professionals

JOY IN WORK

In the play *Bent,* by Martin Sherman (1979), two characters in a Nazi concentration camp are forced to carry rocks from one pile to another all day long. When all of the rocks are on one side, they must move the rocks back to the other side, one by one. One character, Horst, asks Max, the second character, "Why?" Max responds, "It's supposed to drive us crazy . . . it makes no sense. It serves no purpose . . . the work is totally nonessential. I figured it out. They do it to drive us crazy."

Work, to some, is a four-letter word. Others, such as Dr. Schwartz in his "Advice From a Mentor," do not use the term "work" but, instead, refer to their career as a vocation or profession. It may be hard to find joy in a job, which is defined as a task (Cohen, 1994), but most people can find joy in a vocation or profession. Here, we refer to the two words introduced earlier: *intrinsic* and *extrinsic* motivation. If your work is a job that does nothing but bring money or complete a task, this is extrinsic motivation. The characters in *Bent* were extrinsically motivated by threats of death. It is difficult to find joy from extrinsic motivation. But if your work is a profession or vocation and you do it because you really like it or because it is a part of who you are, this is intrinsic motivation.

Some of the values of work, and some of the joys that come from work, are:

a sense of accomplishment

a sense of making a contribution to the world

a sense of helping others

a healthy feeling of being in control of our personal destiny

a sense of belonging to a team

a sense of being productive

a sense of growth and developing one's potential.

Marianne Williamson (1994) sums up the value of work with these words: "The meaning of work, whatever its form, is that it be used to heal the world."

If you find yourself in a profession, a career, or a vocation that turns out to be drudgery and a "job," take the words of Leo Buscaglia (1982) to heart:

If you don't like the scene you're in, if you're unhappy, if you're lonely, if you don't feel things are happening, change your scene. Paint a new backdrop. Surround yourself with new actors. Write a new play—and if it's not a good play, get the hell off the stage and write another one. There are millions of plays—as many as there are people.

JOY IN PEOPLE

From earliest childhood, we have had an idea of what a family does. We learned it from our own parents or from TV shows such as the Waltons, the Brady Bunch, and Bill Cosby. Traditionally, a family has been considered to consist of a mother, father, and their children. Today's family sometimes looks quite different. There may be only one parent, or both parents may be the same sex. Some experts define a family as a group of people who love and support each other in the best and worst of times. Regardless of the biological roots of your family, you can find joy in sharing, giving, and a sense of common history.

Much joy in our lives can come from our friendships. The word itself brings feelings of warmth, comfort, and love. We can find joy in friendship because friendships involve enjoyment, acceptance, trust, respect, mutual assistance, confiding, understanding, and spontaneity. President Woodrow Wilson once said, "Friendship is the only cement that will ever hold the world together." In your new profession, take time to value and nurture existing relationships, and always cultivate new ones.

JOY IN LEISURE

"I wanna hang a big sign around my neck, like daddy's in the barn, 'gone fishin'" (Norman, 1984). Edward Mayo and Lance Jarvis found that Americans spend more than $120 billion annually on leisure-related activities (Cohen, 1994). Much joy can come from leisure activities such as travel, movies, boating, sports, plays, concerts, and just sitting by the lake. Sometimes, however, vacations can be as stressful as going to work. It all depends on how well you are able to relax and let down your guard.

As you begin to seek joy in leisure, you should understand that different leisure activities bring joy to some and stress to others. Some people like to sit on the beach doing nothing during their vacation, and others prefer to be constantly on the move—sightseeing, camping, hiking, or going to museums. Regardless of your preference, as you begin your career, don't underestimate the power of your leisure time. Guard it, protect it, and use it to your best advantage for renewal.

JOY IN GIVING

One of the highest attributes of human potential is the ability to give to the world unselfishly. When we talk about giving, we do not mean material objects or money or possessions. Giving can be as simple as a smile, a compliment, a touch, or a great joke that makes everyone laugh. It is odd that giving is so simple, yet so few seem to have the skill to do so. Kahlil Gibran (1923), in *The Prophet*, says,

> You give little when you give of your possessions. It is when you give of
> yourself that you truly give . . . . There are those who give with joy, and that
> joy is their reward.

It is hard sometimes to understand that each of us, without fail, regardless of age, wisdom, or contribution, are eternally woven into the fabric of this universe. If we were to die at this moment, we could not erase the fact that we played a part in human history. How the pages of that history will read is up to us.

References

Arkoff, Abe. (1995). *The Illuminated Life*. Boston: Allyn and Bacon.

Buscaglia, L. (1982). *Living, Loving and Learning*. New York: Fawcett Columbine.

Chopra, D. (1994). *The Seven Spiritual Laws of Success: A Practical Guide to the Fulfillment of Your Dreams*. San Rafael, CA: Amber-Allen.

Cohen, R. (1994). *Psychology and Adjustment: Values, Culture and Change*. Boston: Allyn and Bacon.

Covey, S. (1989). *The Seven Habits of Highly Effective People: Restoring the Character Ethic*. New York: Simon and Schuster.

Delany, S., and Delany, E., with Hearth, A. (1994). *The Delany Sisters' Book of Everyday Wisdom*. New York: Kodansha International.

Donatelle, Rebecca, and Davis, Lorraine. (1996). *Access to Health* (4th ed.). Boston: Allyn and Bacon.

Gibran, K. (1923). *The Prophet*. New York: Alfred A. Knopf.

Mayo, E., and Jarvis, L. (1981). *The Psychology of Leisure Travel*. Boston: CBI.

Myers, David. (1992). *The Pursuit of Happiness*. New York: Morrow Publishing.

Norman, M. (1983). *Night, Mother*. New York: Avon Books.

Otto, Herbert. (1972). *New Light on Human Potential in Families of the Future*. Ames: Iowa State University Press.

Rogers, Carl. (1961). *On Becoming a Person*. Boston: Houghton Mifflin.

Sherman, Martin. (1979). *Bent*. New York: Avon Books.

Williamson, M. (1994). *Illuminata: A Return to Prayer*. New York: Riverhead Books.

Woolfolk, A. (1998). *Educational Psychology* (7th ed.). Boston: Allyn and Bacon.

CAPSTONES

FOR MAXIMIZING YOUR POTENTIAL

Determine your value system.

▲

Develop a philosophy of life.

▲

Pursue happiness with a passion.

▲

Set and work toward lifelong goals.

▲

Spend time to discover who you are.

▲

Develop your own definition of success.

▲

Spend time reflecting on your life and your potential.

▲

Find joy in work, people, leisure activities, personal growth, and giving.

Creating Balance and Harmony in Your Life

Never feel that your life is frozen in its present routine and that it's hopeless to want anything better. No matter how complicated your life has become, there's a way to unravel it. No matter how many boxes you may be in, there's always a way to pay a price to get out . . . pay the price.

HARRY BROWNE

If you thought that the transition from high school to college was somewhat traumatic and filled with stress, just wait—"You ain't seen nothing yet." Although some people thrive on change and draw their energy from stress, pressure, and deadlines, for most of us, major changes cause a variety of reactions such as fear, guilt, high anxiety, and depression. The transition from college to the world of work, public service, or graduate school will be no different, and you may find it harder to achieve the balance and harmony you need for a healthy lifestyle.

The world in which we live is full of roadblocks that potentially can cause us to lose focus and fall out of balance. Consider the following: Americans reporting that they were "very happy" were no more numerous in 1991 than in 1957. In 1993, only 21 percent of 18- to 29-year-olds think they have a chance at the "good life," compared to 41 percent in 1978. Today, Americans spend 40 percent less time with their children than they did in 1965. Employed Americans spend 163 hours more per year on the job than they did in 1969, and 69 percent of Americans would like to slow down and live a more relaxed life. The typical American household carries $8,570 of non-mortgage personal debt. Seventy percent of Americans say that they would give up a day's pay for a day of free time (*All Consuming Passion,* 1993).

The good news: You can change all of these facts. In an effort to understand what it takes to have a balanced life, this chapter will address the following topics:

▲ A definition of stress

▲ Learning to identify the causes of stress in your life

▲ Developing a stress-reduction plan

▲ Communicating effectively

▲ Managing priorities

▲ Dealing with change

▲ Identifying and using strategies for wellness in the body

▲ Identifying and using strategies for wellness in the mind

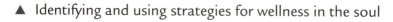

▲ Identifying and using strategies for wellness in the soul

Balance and Harmony in Your Life

The possibility of having balance and harmony in life is not a mythical goal, nor is it a given. Countless books, tapes, and magazines are sold each year with the hope of helping people find some sense of purpose, wellness, and health in their lives. Speakers and writers such as Deepak Chopra and Tony Robins have spoken to tens of thousands of people who want to "have it all." Is it possible? As we explore balance and harmony, you will soon find that the decision is yours.

The Body, Mind, and Soul

A person cannot expect to find balance or harmony unless the body, mind, and soul are working together as one. If your body is well-tuned and your mind is sharp but your soul is hurting, harmony will not be at hand.

In today's world of work, new employees such as yourself can spend upward of 10 to 12 hours per day, 6 days a week on the job. This expectation of employers seems to have become the norm. If you find yourself in such a situation, you are going to have to pay special attention to your body, mind, and soul. Balance and harmony come at a price—a price that many are not willing to pay.

Balance and Harmony in the Body

It has been said that our body is our temple. In today's fast times, however, we tend to forget the importance of taking care of our bodies. One of the most damaging culprits is stress. "Stress" is such a common word that many people do not take it seriously and few understand the dynamic effect that stress can have on the body—not to mention the mind and soul.

The word *stress* comes from the Latin word *strictus,* which means "to draw tight." Stress is your body's reaction to the world around you. Everyone experiences some type of stress. Medical research shows that a certain amount of stress is not bad; in fact, it may even be helpful. Our reaction to stress is what determines if it is good stress (eustress) or bad stress (distress).

As you have worked toward your college degree, you probably have had some physical reactions characteristic of distress such as:

dry mouth	fatigue
tension	impotence
coughs	suicidal thoughts
loss of appetite	insomnia

Distress can have an adverse effect on memory as well. The release of a hormone called cortisol can make you forget things you know you should know (Friend, 1998). "The findings can sometimes explain why the mind goes blank before a key business presentation, a test or an acting debut." This research suggests that it is important to learn how to deal with stress in the body before it becomes overwhelming.

You probably have gone through some positive reactions or eustress as well. Signs of eustress are:

heightened awareness	energy boost
excitement	increased sensitivity
happiness	optimism
liveliness	

As you enter the world of work, no doubt you will experience a plethora of stressful situations. Usually, one, or a combination, of these three elements is causing the stress in your life:

situational stress
psychological stress
biological stress

SITUATIONAL STRESS

Situational stress is the type of stress that comes from the physical or social environment. A change in physical environment, such as moving away from college to accept a job in another region of the country, can cause a great degree of stress. A change in residence, change in work responsibilities, change in living conditions, and revision of personal habits all appear on the Holmes-Rahe Scale (1967), which measures life-event stresses.

Social-environmental stress is a result of people around you changing. You probably will experience this as you complete your degree and move on to the world of work. You will have new friends, new colleagues, and new neighbors. Completing school, change in living conditions, and change in social activities appear on the Holmes-Rahe Scale.

▲ ▲ ▲

PSYCHOLOGICAL STRESS

As you begin to look for a job, prepare a resume, get ready for graduation, rent a moving truck, and buy airline tickets for job interviews, you may begin to feel psychological stress. This is stress caused by events.

▲ ▲ ▲

BIOLOGICAL STRESS

Biological stress is caused by new, physical demands on your body. While in college, you may have opted to take classes that began after 10:00 A.M. Your new job may require you to be at work by 8:00 A.M., and you may have to stay after 5:00 P.M. This can cause stress on your physical body.

Stress-Reduction Plan for the Body

Instead of letting stress get the best of your body, you can do some things to prevent or alleviate stress. We suggest trying one, or a combination, of the following:

1. **Relaxation techniques** Relaxation techniques can be as simple as closing your office door or looking away from your computer for 5 minutes, closing your eyes, taking deep breaths, or listening to soothing music. You don't have to be an expert in yoga to relax, and this may be something that you want to explore also.

2. **Exercise** You don't have to belong to an expensive gym to get enough exercise to reduce stress in you body. Exercise can be as easy as walking around the office building to stretching at your desk. Some people use part of their lunch break to do moderate exercise.

3. **Massage therapy** Many people think they have to be on vacation to enjoy the benefits of a massage. This is not true. Though it is hard to find the time or the money to go to a formal massage therapist daily or weekly, this can be seen as a reward for a job well done. If you know you are going to be involved in a stressful project, you may want to prearrange

one or more massages during the project span. In the meantime, you may find relief in a simple neck, shoulder, or back rub from your spouse, significant other, or friend.

4. **Aroma Therapy** Millions of dollars are spent yearly on various aromas that elicit emotions or feelings. We've all had a moment when we caught a whiff of some perfume or cologne that brought back memories of something or someone pleasant. Aroma therapy works much the same way. You don't have to have expensive equipment or a lab to mix formulas. You can practice aroma therapy in your office, your car, or your home.

5. **Healthy Eating Habits** Sometimes, one of the hardest things to do when we get into a new situation is to maintain a healthy diet. It can be as easy as stopping to think about your food choices. Grabbing a fast-food snack at lunch or dinner may seem to be a handy solution, but this may represent a meal loaded with fat, cholesterol, and calories.

6. **Holistic Care** Just as it would be difficult to achieve balance and harmony without considering the body, mind, and soul together, it probably will be just as difficult to

ADVICE FROM A MENTOR

Steve Spearman,

Vice President for Retail Education
Bank One, Dallas, TX

Somebody has to remain calm. The first weeks of our bank conversion, we were managing 33 trainers at seven sites; this had never been done before. It was not that my insides were not torn up, but I had to remain calm on the outside. It is almost like the poised flight attendant when the plane is taking a nose dive. Someone has to be there, smiling and calm. I take a deep breath, think about the situation, and ask myself, "Is this bad enough to make us shut down the project?" If the answer is no, I can make it work. I have to put things into perspective and prioritize the tasks to be done.

In college, there are many requirements that can cause stress. You only have one semester to complete the tasks described in the syllabus; they

must be done. The world of work is much the same. One must learn how to manage time to accomplish the things required. I have learned that I can set priorities or I can try to play catch-up at the very end. I chose to set priorities. On my job today, I almost make a syllabus for each major project. This helps control my stress level.

maintain a healthy body by following just one of the above tips. With the demands of today's workplace, you may have to practice a variety of the techniques presented in this chapter.

Balance and Harmony in the Mind

As we strive for balance and harmony in our lives, we also must consider the mind—how we think, how we make decisions, how we communicate, and how we plan for the future. The loss of balance and harmony in the mind usually comes from one or all of three factors: poor communication efforts (discussed in Chapter 5), the inability to set realistic priorities, and an unwillingness or inability to change. These three situations can be controlled, but a great deal of effort is necessary to manage all three simultaneously. First, review Chapter 5 to refresh your mind about communication. Then learn how to set priorities and deal with change, discussed next.

▲ ▲ ▲

MANAGING PRIORITIES

If you were to ask most people in today's workplace, they would tell you that they simply do not have enough time to get everything done that is required of them in one day. Some would tell you that the phone, computer, Internet, faxes, mail, and meetings cloud their days. Others would tell you that they are able to accomplish all that has to be done. Still others, if they are honest, would tell you that they simply don't know how to set priorities. The truth of matter is that priority management is a personal and independent thing. No one priority management plan will fit every person.

Some priority-management experts suggest

ADVICE CONTINUED.

I'd like to say that I have a wonderful system for managing the information that comes to me. I don't. I don't have a perfect office. work out of conference rooms, cubicles, or someone else's office. In the middle of the project, it would be great to say that I answer email at 10, 12, and 2. That can't happen in the course of my regular day.

My advice to you as you enter the world of work is this: It is not anything like you ever imagined. The world of work is constantly changing. When you began your studies, the world was one way. Because of rapid change and technology, it is now different, very different. You have to learn how to change, how to keep up, and how to move with the flow.

that you list your priorities and check them off as you go through the day. This works for a great many professionals. Others buy day planners to manage their days. This, too, works for some. Other experts suggest that you let your assistant plan your calendar and activities. Again, this plan works for some.

A study of top executives and their daily work habits and priority-management efforts revealed that "most of their time wasn't planned in advance" (Deutschman, 1992). It was found that they spent 76 percent of their time talking to others. "The country's top executives walk into the office in the morning with only a vague sense of what the day will bring."

When it comes to managing your priorities, you have to sort out what style best fits you, your company, and your life. The following tips on priority management may help you develop your own management plan:

- Instead of writing memos, use the telephone or email whenever possible.
- Learn to say no.
- Avoid scheduling meetings whenever possible. Will a phone call or email do?
- Clean off your desk daily.
- Never handle correspondence twice.
- Reply directly on memos and letters.
- Learn to delegate when possible.
- Study yourself to find out what hours of the day you are most productive and use that time wisely.
- Develop a daily to-do list and see if this works for you.
- Carry a small notepad with you at all times.
- Focus on completing one task at a time if possible.
- Leave your work area during lunch.
- Make your work area fit your style—make it stimulating and fun.
- Work on harder projects first.
- Don't schedule back-to-back meetings if you can help it; leave time to process the previous meeting.

DEALING WITH CHANGE

The enduring phrase "nothing endures but change" was written by Heraclitus, a Greek philosopher, more than 2,500 years ago. If he only could have envisioned the technological changes in the past 100 years alone, his statement might have read, "Nothing endures but change—and our inability to keep pace with it."

Some of the most successful and happy people in the world today are those who have learned that change is constant and change can be good. In a survey of centenarians, one of the only commonalities found as to why they lived more than 100 years was their ability to deal with change. Maintaining balance and harmony in your life may very well depend on how well, and how quickly, you learn to deal with the changes in your workplace and in the world in general.

Why is there so much change? Why can't things stay the same? The answer in the business world is: Change or die. Consider the following results brought about by change: Ford Motor Company achieved a 75 percent productivity improvement in its accounts payable process. Milliken achieved an 89 percent improvement in filling custom orders. Citicorp achieved a 67 percent improvement in processing mortgage applications. Toyota achieved a 40 percent improvement in product development (Development Dimensions International, 1994). Had these companies not changed to meet the demands of the market, they probably would not have survived.

The same answer as to why businesses change might be true for you personally. Although you would not literally die, your career and opportunities might. Just 5 to 7 years ago, we could not conceive that there would be lucrative careers called Web Masters. And 10 to 15 years ago, it would have been inconceivable that work as a fabric weaver in the textile industry would nearly vanish from the U. S. labor force. Change happens.

As you begin to develop your plan to achieve and maintain balance in your life, consider the following tips for dealing with change:

- View change as a growth opportunity.
- Give change a chance; it could be the best thing that ever happened to you.
- Get involved with the change; don't just let it happen to you; guide it along and have an open mind.
- Learn to let go.
- Develop a sense of humor.
- Keep the lines of communication open.
- Focus on the outcome. Will life be better after the change?
- Learn as much as possible about the change.
- Teach as much as possible about the change.
- Stay positive; avoid negative rumors and gossip.

Balance and Harmony in the Soul

As strange as it may seem to talk about one's soul, we absolutely must consider the condition of our soul when discussing balance and harmony in our life. As long as there has been recorded history, philosophers, religious figures, leaders, and lay people have labored over the meaning of *soul* and just how much attention should be paid to something that can't be seen or touched. Few agree as to the answers.

Thomas Moore (1992) says:

> The soul is not a thing, but a quality or a dimension of experiencing life and ourselves. It has to do with depth, value, relatedness, heart, and personal substance.

He suggests that we can't care for our soul until we discover how it operates in each of us. For some, the soul blossoms when it witnesses beauty. For others, it flourishes when friends are near. Some are enriched by giving, and others by receiving. Each soul operates differently, and each person must care for his or her own soul in his or her own unique way.

It has been said that we are lucky if we have one or two close, personal friends—soulmates if you will—over the years of our lives. Ironically, most people list friendship and relationships as one of the most important ingredients in a happy and healthy life. Medical research suggests that positive relationships with people are paramount. Evidence suggests that an absence of satisfying communication and interaction can even jeopardize life itself. For instance:

> Socially isolated people are two to three times more likely to die prematurely than are those with strong social ties. The type of communication relationship does not seem to matter; marriages, friendships, and community ties all seem to increase longevity. Divorced men (before the age of 70) die from heart diseases, cancer, and strokes at double the rate of married men. Three times as many die from hypertension; five times as many commit suicide; seven times as many die from cirrhosis of the liver; and ten times as many die from tuberculosis. The rate of all types of cancer is as much as five times higher for divorced men and women compared to their counterparts. (Adler et al., 1989)

Clearly, to achieve some balance and harmony, the soul needs other people. As we care for the soul, we should consider that every moment spent with friends and significant others could be the moment that we find happiness and, in all frankness, the last moment we may share with them. Deepak Chopra (1994) says:

> We have stopped for a moment to encounter each other, to meet, to love, to share. This is a precious moment, but it is transient. It is a little parenthesis in eternity. If we share with caring, lightheartedness, and love, we will create abundance and joy for each other. And then this moment will have been worthwhile.

As you work to maintain balance and harmony in your life, consider the following ways to nurture you soul:

- Develop an appreciation of, and participate in, the fine arts.
- Make time for heart-to-heart conversations with friends and loved ones.
- Take stock of your value system and work to maintain harmony with those values.
- Devote time to your own spirituality.
- Laugh often.
- Cry as much as you need to.
- Apologize when you should.
- Forgive yourself.
- Support yourself with positive, upbeat people.
- Reward yourself.
- Take long walks and enjoy nature.
- Listen to all types of music. Sing in the car.
- Play an honest, fair game in a sporting event.
- Give as much love, honesty, trust, and compassion as you can. It will come back to you.
- Spend time with yourself and develop your own life philosophy.
- Make a commitment to live by that philosophy.
- Celebrate your strengths.
- Take a positive risk each day.

References

Adler, R., Lawrence, R., and Townde, N. (1989). *Interplay: The Process of Interpersonal Communication.* New York: Holt, Rinehart & Winston.

Chopra, D. (1994). *The Seven Spiritual Laws of Success: A Practical Guide to the Fulfillment of Your Dreams.* San Rafael, CA: Amber-Allen Publishing.

Deutschman, A. (1992). The CEO's Secret of Managing Time. *Fortune,* June 1, Vol. 125, No. 11.

Development Dimensions International. (1994). *Making Re-engineering Work.* Atlanta: PEPI Conference Re-engineering Forum.

Friend, T. (1998). The Effects of Stress. *USA Today,* Aug. 20.

Holmes, T., and Rahe, R. (1967). The Social Readjustment Scale. *Journal of Psychosomatic Research,* Vol. 11, No. 2.

Krackhardt, D., and Hanson, J. (1993). Informal Networks: The Company Behind the Chart. *Harvard Business Review,* July–August.

Moore, Thomas. (1992). *Care of the Soul: A Guide for Cultivating Depth and Sacredness in Everyday Life.* New York: Harper Perennial.

New Road Map Foundation. (1993). *All Consuming Passion: Waking Up From the American Dream* (2d ed.). New Road Map Foundation.

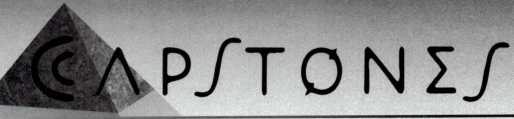

CAPSTONES

FOR MAINTAINING BALANCE AND HARMONY

Be proactive in your life.

▲

Learn to manage priorities.

▲

Work to reduce stress in your life.

▲

Develop your own ideas of success.

▲

Develop positive communication skills.

▲

Strive to understand and embrace change.

▲

Develop and live by your own life philosophy.

▲

Maintain positive relationships personally and professionally.

▲

Live the life you want to live, not one that others dictate.

▲

Choose to be a lifelong learner.

Index